OPERATING
INSTRUCTIONS

ALSO BY ANNE LAMOTT

Hard Laughter

Rosie

Joe Jones

All New People

OPERATING INSTRUCTIONS

*A Journal of
My Son's First Year*

ANNE LAMOTT

PANTHEON BOOKS
New York and San Francisco

The Preface of this work was originally published in slightly different form in
Focus Magazine.

Grateful acknowledgment is made to the following for permission to reprint
previously published material:

Alfred A. Knopf, Inc.: excerpt from "Thirteen ways of Looking at a Blackbird"
from *The Collected Poems of Wallace Stevens* by Wallace Stevens. Copyright 1923
and renewed 1951 by Wallace Stevens. Reprintd by permission of Alfred A.
Knopf, Inc. Rights in the British Commonwealth administered by Faber &
Faber, Ltd.

Random House, Inc.: adaptation of excerpt from "Sonnets to Orpheus" in *Selected
Poetry of Rainer Maria Rilke,* edited and translated by Stephen Mitchell. Copyright
© 1982 by Stephen Mitchell. Reprinted by permission of Random House, Inc.

Library of Congress Cataloging-in-Publication Data

Lamott, Anne.
    Operating instructions / Anne Lamott.
      p.   cm.
    ISBN 0-679-42091-6
    I. Title.
    PS3562.A4645S26   1993
    813'.54—dc20   92-30540

Book design by Jan Melchior
Manufactured in the United States of America

9 8 7 6 5 4

*This one
is for
Pamela Murray,
and
Sam Lamott*

SEAL LULLABY

Oh! hush thee, my baby, the night is behind us,
  And black are the waters that sparkled so green.

• • •

The storm shall not wake thee, no shark overtake thee,
  Asleep in the arms of the slow-swinging seas.

—RUDYARD KIPLING

Acknowledgments

It's hard to know where to begin. This book would not exist if my old agent, Abby Thomas, had not more or less insisted that I type up the journal I kept of my son's first year. Come to think of it, the journal would not have existed if my friend John Manning had not insisted, while I was pregnant, that after Sam's arrival I write down a few observations about him every single day. I am deeply grateful to these two people.

I want to thank my editor at Pantheon, Jack Shoemaker, for his faith and commitment and tireless efforts, and also my new agent, Chuck Verrill. John Curley, John Kaye, Don Carpenter, Donna Levin, Steve Barclay, Neshama Franklin, Cindy Ehrlich, Jane Vandenburgh, and especially Steve Lamott always offer immeasurable support and insight, even let me sometimes steal their lines.

Julie and John Woodbridge were there for me a thousand times that first year, as was my beloved reading group—Orville Schell, Deirdre English, Adam Hochschild, John Krich, Larry Friedlander, Lizzie Ehmann, Ethan Canin, and Sedge Thomson. It's odd that Sue August's name does not turn up frequently in these pages, for she is always a devoted and insightful friend. Mary Turnbull and Alice Adams have been so loving and generous with both me and Sam for so long that I don't think I can capture my feelings in words. And I would not still be here at all without the support and love of the people of Saint Andrew Presbyterian Church, Marin City, California.

Someone somewhere quoted a line from an old *New Yorker* story to the effect that we are not here to see through one another, but to see one another through. This is so much what the aforementioned people, and the main characters in this book, have done for me.

OPERATING
INSTRUCTIONS

SOME THOUGHTS ON BEING PREGNANT:
A PREFACE OF SORTS

I woke up with a start at 4:00 one morning and realized that I was very, very pregnant. Since I had conceived six months earlier, one might have thought that the news would have sunk in before then, and in many ways it had, but it was on that early morning in May that I first realized how severely pregnant I was. What tipped me off was that, lying on my side and needing to turn over, I found myself unable to move. My first thought was that I had had a stroke.

Nowadays I go around being aware that I am pregnant with the same constancy and lack of surprise with which I go around being aware that I have teeth. But a few times a day the information actually causes me to gasp—how on earth did I come to be in this condition? Well, I have a few suspicions. I mean, I am beginning to put two and two together. See, there was this guy. But the guy is no longer around, and my stomach is noticeably bigger every few days.

I could have had an abortion—the pressure to do so was extraordinary—and if need be, I would take to the streets, armed, to defend the right of any woman for any reason to terminate a pregnancy, but I was totally unable to do so this time psychologically, psychically, emotionally. Just totally. So I am going to have a baby pretty soon, and this has raised some mind-boggling issues.

For instance, it occurs to me over and over that I am much too self-centered, cynical, eccentric, and edgy to raise a baby, especially alone. (The baby's father was dramatically less excited than I was to find out I was pregnant, so much so that I have not seen or heard from him in months and don't expect to ever again.) At thirty-five years old, I may be too old and too tired to be having my first child. And I really *did* think for several seconds that I might have had a stroke; it is not second nature for me to believe that everything is more or less okay. Clearly, my nerves are shot.

For example, the other day one of the innumerable deer that come down here from the mountain to eat in the garden and drink from the stream remained where it was as I got closer and closer. It was standing between me and my front door. I thought, Boy, they're getting brazen, and I walked closer and closer to it, finally to within four or five feet, when suddenly it tensed. My first thought was that it was about to lunge at me, snarling. Of course it turned instead and bolted through the woods, but I was left with the increasingly familiar sense that I am losing my grasp on reality.

One moment I'm walking along the salt marsh listening to

4

sacred choral music on headphones, convinced that the music is being piped in through my ears, into my head, down my throat, and into my torso where the baby will be able to hear it, and the next moment I'm walking along coaching the baby on how best to grow various body parts. What are you, some kind of *nut?* I ask myself, and I know the answer is yes, *some* kind of nut, and maybe one who is not well enough to be a mother. But this is not the worst fear.

Even the three weeks of waiting for the results of the amniocentesis weren't the most fearful part, nor was the amnio itself. It was, in fact, one of the sweetest experiences of my life. My friend Manning drove me into San Francisco and stayed with me through the procedure, and, well, talk about intimate. It made sex look like a game of Twister. I lay there on the little table at the hospital with my stomach sticking out, Manning near my head holding my hands, a nurse by my feet patting me from time to time, one doctor running the ultrasound device around and around the surface of my tummy, the other doctor taking notes until it was his turn with the needles.

The ultrasound doctor was showing me the first pictures of my baby, who was at that point a four-month-old fetus. He was saying, "Ah, there's the head now . . . there's the leg . . . there's its bottom," and I was watching it all on the screen, nodding, even though it was all just underwater photography, all quite ethereal and murky. Manning said it was like watching those first men on the moon. I pretended to be able to

5

distinguish each section of the baby because I didn't want the doctor to think I was a lousy mother who was already judging the kid for not being photogenically distinct enough. He pointed out the vertebrae, a sweet curved strand of pearls, and then the heart, beating as visibly as a pulsar, and that was when I started to cry.

Then the other doctor took one of his needles and put it right through my stomach, near my belly button, in a circle that the ultrasound doctor had described with the end of a straw. I felt a pinch, and then mild cramping, and that was all, as the doctor began to withdraw some amniotic fluid. Now you probably think, like I thought, that this fluid is some vaguely holy saltwater, flown in from the coast for the occasion, but it is mostly baby pee, light green in color. What they do with it then is to send it to the lab, where they culture it, growing enough cells from the tissue the baby has sloughed off into the amniotic fluid to determine if there are chromosomal abnormalities and whether it is a boy or a girl, if you care to know.

During the first week of waiting, you actually believe your baby is okay, because you saw it scoot around during the ultrasound and because most babies are okay. By the middle of the second week, things are getting a bit dicey in your head, but most of the time you still think the baby is okay. But on the cusp of the second and third weeks, you come to know—

not to believe but to know—that you are carrying a baby inside you in only the broadest sense of the word *baby*, because what is growing in there has a head the size of a mung bean, with almost no brain at all because all available tissue has gone into the building of a breathtaking collection of arms and knees—maybe not too many arms but knees absolutely *everywhere*.

Finally, though, the nurse who had patted my feet during the amnio called, and the first thing she said was that she had good news, and I thought I might actually throw up from sheer joy. Then she talked about the findings for a while, although I did not hear a word, and then she said, "Do you want to know its sex?" And I said yes I did.

It is a boy. His name is Sam Lamott. Samuel John Stephen Lamott. (My brothers' names are John and Steve.)

A boy. Do you know what that means? Do you know what boys have that girls don't? That's right, there you go. They have penises. And like most of my women friends, I have somewhat mixed feelings about this. Now, I don't know how to put this delicately, but I have never been quite the same since seeing a penis up close while I was on LSD years and years ago. It was an actual penis; I mean, it wasn't like I was staring at my hand for an hour and watched it turn into my grandfather's face and then into a bat and then into a penis. It was the real thing. It was my boyfriend's real thing, and what it looked like was the root of all my insanity, of a lot of my suffering and obsession. It looked like a cross between a snake and a heart.

That is a really intense thing you boys have there, and we internal Americans of the hetero persuasion have really, really conflicted feelings about you external Americans because of the way you wield those things, their power over us, and especially their power over you. I ask you once again to remember the old joke in which the puzzled, defensive man says, "*I* didn't want to go to Las Vegas," then points to his crotch and says, "*He* wanted to go to Las Vegas." So it has given me pause to learn that there is a baby boy growing in my belly who apparently has all the right number of hands and feet and arms and legs and knees, a normal-size head, and a penis.

Penises are so—what is the word?—*funky.* They're wonderful, too, and I love them, but over the years such bad things have happened to me because of them. I've gotten pregnant, even when I tried so hard not to, and I've gotten diseases, where you couldn't see any evidence of disease on the man's dick and he claims not to have anything, but you end up having to get treatment and it's totally humiliating and weird, and the man's always mad at you for having caught it, even though you haven't slept with anyone else for months or even years. It is my secret belief that men love their penises so much that when they take them in to show their doctors, after their women claim to have caught a little something, the male doctors get caught up in this penis love, whack the patient (your lover) on the back, and say thunderously, "Now don't be silly, that's a *damn* fine penis you've got there."

A man told me once that all men like to look at themselves in the mirror when they're hard, and now I keep picturing Sam in twenty years, gazing at his penis in the mirror while feeling psychologically somewhere between Ivan Boesky and Mickey Mantle. I also know he will be someone who will one day pee with pride, because all men do, standing there manfully tearing bits of toilet paper to shreds with their straight and forceful sprays, carrying on as if this were one of history's great naval battles—the Battle of Midway, for instance. So of course I'm a little edgy about the whole thing, about my child having a penis instead of a nice delicate little lamb of a vagina. But even so, this is still not the worst fear.

No, the worst thing, worse even than sitting around crying about that inevitable day when my son will leave for college, worse than thinking about whether or not in the meantime to get him those hideous baby shots he probably should have but that some babies die from, worse than the fears I have when I lie awake at 3:00 in the morning (that I won't be able to make enough money and will have to live in a tenement house where the rats will bite our heads while we sleep, or that I will lose my arms in some tragic accident and will have to go to court and diaper my son using only my mouth and feet and

9

the judge won't think I've done a good enough job and will put Sam in a foster home), worse even than the fear I feel whenever a car full of teenagers drives past my house going 200 miles an hour on our sleepy little street, worse than thinking about my son being run over by one of those drunken teenagers, or of his one day becoming one of those teenagers— worse than just about anything else is the agonizing issue of how on earth anyone can bring a child into this world knowing full well that he or she is eventually going to have to go through the seventh and eighth grades.

The seventh and eighth grades were for me, and for every single good and interesting person I've ever known, what the writers of the Bible meant when they used the words *hell* and *the pit*. Seventh and eighth grades were a place into which one descended. One descended from the relative safety and wild-ness and bigness one felt in sixth grade, eleven years old. Then the worm turned, and it was all over for any small feeling that one was essentially all right. One wasn't. One was no longer just some kid. One was suddenly a Diane Arbus character. It was springtime, for Hitler, and Germany.

I experienced it as being a two-year game of "The Farmer in the Dell." I hung out with the popular crowd, as jester, but boy, when those parties and dances rolled round, this cheese stood alone, watching my friends go steady and kiss, and then, like all you other cheeses, I went home and cried. There we were, all of us cheeses alone, emotionally broken by unrequited love and at the same time amped out of our minds on hormones and shame.

Seventh and eighth grades were about waiting to get picked for teams, waiting to get asked to dance, waiting to grow taller, waiting to grow breasts. They were about praying for God to grow dark hairs on my legs so I could shave them. They were about having pipe-cleaner legs. They were about violence, meanness, chaos. They were about *The Lord of the Flies.* They were about feeling completely other. But more than anything else, they were about hurt and aloneness. There is a beautiful poem by a man named Roy Fuller, which ends, "Hurt beyond hurting, never to forget," and whenever I remember those lines, which is often, I think of my father's death ten years ago this month, and I think about seventh and eighth grades.

So how on earth can I bring a child into the world, knowing that such sorrow lies ahead, that it is such a large part of what it means to be human?

I'm not sure. That's my answer: I'm not sure. One thing I do know is that I've recently been through it again, the total aloneness in the presence of almost extraterrestrially high levels of hormones. I have been thinking a lot lately of Phil Spector and his Wall of Sound, because to be pregnant is to be backed by a wall of hormones, just like during puberty, and the sense of aloneness that goes along with that is something I have been dancing as fast as I could to avoid ever having to feel again.

For the last twenty-some years, I have tried everything in sometimes suicidally vast quantities—alcohol, drugs, work, food, excitement, good deeds, popularity, men, exercise, and just rampant compulsion and obsession—to avoid having to be in the same room with that sense of total aloneness. And I did pretty well, although I nearly died. But then recently that aloneness walked right into my house without knocking, sat down, and stayed a couple of weeks.

In those two weeks, tremendous amounts of support poured in, as did baby clothes and furniture. My living room started to look like a refugee relocation center, but the aloneness was here, too, and it seemed to want to be felt. I was reminded once again that the people closest to me, including my therapist, function as my pit crew, helping me to fix blown-out tires and swabbing me off between laps, and the consensus, among those individuals who make up my pit crew, was that I was probably just going to have to go ahead and feel the aloneness for a while. So I did, and I'll tell you it didn't feel very good. But somehow I was finally able to stand in that huge open wound and feel it and acknowledge it because it was real, and the fear of the pain of this wound turned out to be worse than the actual pain.

As I said, though, it didn't feel very good, and it brought me up against that horrible, hateful truth—that there wasn't anything outside myself that could heal or fill me and that everything I had been running from and searching for all my life was within. So I sat with those things for a while, and the wounds began to heal.

This all took place a few months ago, at age thirty-five. I mean, I'm old and tough and I can take it. But Sam is just a baby. Sam, in fact, hasn't even come out of the chute yet. I guess when he does, there will be all these people to help him along on his journey; he will have his pit crews, too, but at some point he will also have to start seventh grade. Maybe he will be one of those kids who get off easy, but probably not. I don't know many who did. So he will find himself at some point, maybe many times, in what feels like a crawl space, scared of unseen spiders, pulling himself along on his elbows, the skin rubbed raw, not knowing for sure whether he will ever arrive at a place where he can stand up again in the daylight. This is what it feels like to grieve a loss that is just too big, the loss of a loved one, or of one's childhood, or whatever. (And it is sometimes what it feels like to be in the middle of writing a book; and also what it feels like sometimes when you've lost your hormonal equilibrium.)

Yet we almost always come out on the other side, maybe not with all our *f-a-c-u-l-t-i-e-s* intact, as Esmé put it, but in good enough shape. I was more or less okay by ninth grade. I am more or less okay now. I really love my pit crew, and I sometimes love my work. Sometimes it feels like God has reached down and touched me, blessed me a thousand times over, and sometimes it all feels like a mean joke, like God's advisers are Muammar Qaddafi and Phyllis Schlafly.

So I am often awake these days in the hours before the dawn, full of joy, full of fear. The first birds begin to sing at quarter after five, and when Sam moves around in my stomach, kicking, it feels like there are trout inside me, leaping, and I go in and out of the aloneness, in and out of that sacred place.

S E P T E M B E R   7 ,   1 9 8 9

So anyway, I had a baby last week. The night before, my best friend Pammy took me to the city because I was having cramps, and it turned out I was in the earliest possible labor—quite effaced but barely dilated a centimeter. Pammy and I had gone through Lamaze training together—actually we've gone through the last twenty-five years together, through our teens and through my dad's death in my early twenties, and through her ten-year marriage, which has been a happy one, and through my getting clean and sober in my early thirties, and most recently through my pregnancy and Lamaze. Pammy is so beautiful, a natural platinum blonde with blue eyes and the most engaging, brilliant, kind, and funny mind. You would never believe that her parents were the two worst falling-down drunks you ever saw. I remember, as a teenager, stepping over her mother, Mary, at 9:00 in the morning. She'd have passed out an hour earlier on the living room floor, and then you'd meet up with her at breakfast and act nonchalant about the whole thing, like "Hi, Mary, want some toast?" Her father was this violent, crazy, Irish drunk, who murdered his mother's best friend when Pammy was thirteen. But Pammy is unquestionably the sanest, most grounded and giving person I've ever known. She plays classical piano and flute and makes a living doing these stunning blown-glass figurines for boutiques and street fairs, and she's been my guardian for years and years now. I've always secretly wondered if my family has been slipping her a small salary over the years to take me for our daily walks and keep an eye on things.

Anyway, after the doctor told us to go home that night, we were driving across the Golden Gate Bridge back to Marin, feeling giddy and afraid because it was maybe really happening, and we both got worried that we wouldn't remember anything from Lamaze. I was suddenly panicked about not having enough Q-tips or diaper wipes. She asked how I was feeling, now that I was officially dilated one centimeter, and I replied that it was really all I could do not to start pushing the baby out right there in the car.

Early the next morning, after having been up all night together at my house timing my contractions and watching *That's Entertainment* on TV, we drove back into the city, and I thought I was about to deliver, but the male doctor who examined me at Kaiser said I was only dilated two centimeters and couldn't be admitted, although I was in real pain by then. I went into a terrible, fearful depression. The doctor looked at the baby's heartbeat on the monitor and said dully, "The

baby's flat," and I instantly assumed it meant he was dead or
at least retarded from lack of oxygen. I don't think a woman
doctor would ever say anything like that to a mother. "Flat?"
I said incredulously. _"Flat?"_ Then he explained that this meant
the baby was in a sleep cycle. So Pammy and I ended up
walking up and down Geary Boulevard trying to get me to
dilate more, and we were actually laughing quite a lot intermittently. I called my brother Steve, who is five years younger than
I, and asked him to please come be with us. I told him we were
pretty worn-out and needed fresh horses. He said he'd come
as fast as he could. Pammy and I continued down Geary,
stopping in at Mel's Drive-in, with me panting my way
through contractions like a dog. I'll tell you, we got served
very, very quickly. I had a bowl of oatmeal.

When we got back to Kaiser, I was dilated enough for
admission, but there were no birthing rooms available, and I
got so incredibly depressed again that I felt about ten years old.
Kaiser sent us over to Mount Zion Hospital; they offered us
an ambulance, but I was too depressed and pissed off and
wanted to punish them, so I wouldn't let them help me.
Pammy drove and I was bellowing at the top of my lungs the
entire way. There was blood all down the back of my dress
when we got out of the car, and Pammy said really nicely, "Oh,
it's not bad, it just looks like a little crankcase oil."

Life became a whole lot better at Mount Zion. Both the
nurses who were taking care of me had read my books and

were treating me like I was Princess Di. The doctor was a woman and I fell in love with her, and I felt really for the first time that things were going to be okay. Perhaps there was a fifty-fifty chance that I would actually give birth to a live baby. I got the epidural immediately and decided that next time, if there is a next time, I will get the epidural upon registration. Lamaze is great and the classes totally educated Pammy and me about what to expect, but I never intended to have a natural childbirth. The moment that epidurals were mentioned in our class, Pammy and I had turned to each other and nodded. I had a few great hours of heavy but epiduralized labor. Then it became hard at the end, and everything went wrong. I couldn't push the baby out, and Pammy and Steve stood by my feet in the labor room for an hour, exhorting, encouraging me to push, telling me how beautifully I was doing. I was in despair. I made a tiny little poo on the table, which they didn't mention at the time but which they now manage to work into about two-thirds of all our conversations. I believe that when the last nail is being hammered into my coffin, they will both be peering in, saying, "Oh, remember when she made that little tiny poo on the table when she was having Sam?" And then I got really sick. I got an infection from where Sam's fist tore a little hole in my vagina. (He came out with his fist balled up by the side of his head. I'm reasonably sure he was trying to do the black-power salute.) I was shivering like a wet dog and felt like I was freezing to death even though I had a big fever by then. The nurse kept covering me with sheets that she'd just taken out of a dryer. The doctor, Carol Gerdes, who was a resident, stayed way after her shift was over because she knew I felt safe with her. I kept saying, "But you only get one weekend off a *month*, you really should go home now," and she'd say, "Do you want me to stay?" And I'd think for a second and then say, "Yes."

Finally, finally, Sam slid out, and they put him on my chest for a bit and then cleaned him up, and then Pammy and Steve held him because I was too hurt and out of it. They walked around the room with him, explaining what various things were and that he would get used to the light. They'd bring him over to me every few minutes and then carry him around again when I was too preoccupied with the fever and the stitching. I felt like my heart was going to break from all the mixed-up feelings and because I couldn't even really take care of my baby. Finally the fever went away, just as the doctor finished stitching me up, and hope came back into me, hope and tremendous feelings of buoyancy and joy.

They took us all to my room, Sam and Pammy and Steve and me, and I nursed the baby for the first time. None of us could take our eyes off him. He was the most beautiful thing I had ever seen. He was like moonlight.

Sam is two weeks old today. His umbilical cord fell off. I'm probably supposed to feel like the cord is very lovely and natural, but I must say I'm going to be able to live without it somehow. It's like something a long-haired cat would get stuck in her tail.

Sam is unbelievably pretty, with long, thin, Christlike feet. I told my friend Carpenter this and he said, "It's an often-difficult world out there, and it's good to have long, grippy feet." I've decided the reason Sam's so gorgeous is that God knew that I wouldn't have been able to fall in love with this shitting and colicky little bundle if he looked like one of those E.T./Don Rickles babies.

I'm crazy tired. I feel as stressed out by exhaustion as someone who spent time in Vietnam. Maybe mothers who have husbands or boyfriends do not get so savagely exhausted, but I doubt it. They probably end up with these eccentric babies *plus* Big Foot skulking around the house pissed off because the mom is too tired to balance his checkbook or give him a nice blow job.

This is strictly sour grapes. I wish I had a husband. I wish Sam had a dad. I hope God sends him one someday. It is a huge thing not to have. Some friends of mine are having a baby in a couple of months, and they already know it is a boy and that he has only one whole arm, which of course is also a huge thing not to have. They are also going to call their baby Sam. The other Sam's father and I were both teaching at a writing conference in Napa a month ago, right before I delivered. I was massively pregnant, looking and feeling like a skinny ugly teenager with a giant baby in her tum. Even the oldest black people at my church had been laughing when they saw me the week before. The other Sam's father and I were floating around a swimming pool, and I was thinking about how sad I feel sometimes because my dad is dead and he won't ever get to know Sam, at least on this funny blue marble. Then I got sad because Sam wasn't going to have some Alan Alda/Hugh Beaumont dad hanging around, throwing him up into the air and teaching him how to do manly things, like how to pee standing up and how to fix the toaster oven. Thinking about the other Sam without much of a left arm and of course no left hand, my chest just ached. I pictured the two Sams at the fiction workshop the following year, hanging out together while we taught our classes, and my Sam studying the other Sam and saying, "So where's your arm?" and the other baby shrugging and saying, "I don't know; where's your dad?"

There are a couple of things I want to remember about Sam's earlier days, his youth, now that he's kind of an old guy with no umbilical cord. The first thing happened the day my friend Peg and I brought him home from the hospital, during what for me felt like the most harrowing ride a person could take through San Francisco. The first time we hit a pothole, I thought, Well, that's that, his neck just snapped; we broke him. He's a quadriplegic now. But we did get him home safely, and Pammy was there to greet us.

She and Peg are Sam's godmothers. Peg is big and athletic and deeply spiritual, sober in Alcoholics Anonymous for three years now. Toward the end of her drinking and using, she'd done so much cocaine one night that she woke up in a motel in Monterey with her face glued to the pillow by all the blood that had poured out of her nose while she slept. But she still didn't think she had a real problem, and she didn't get clean for another few months. I *like* that in a girl. That's pretty much how I was. Whereas Pammy, with these two hideous falling-down-drunk parents, has a couple of glasses of wine every few nights, and maybe pours a third glass, and then leaves most of it. That used to drive me crazy. It would seem like an act of aggression. I'd ask, "Why don't you finish that wine?" and she'd say, "I just don't really want it," and I'd ask why, and she'd say, "I'm already starting to *feel* it," and I'd look at her like I was going to have to take her back to the asylum in the morning.

Anyway, being there with Sam and Pammy and Peg was a dream come true, except that I was also having little blips of fear. I had all these nightmare images, left over from the last few months of my pregnancy, of what a petri dish my house was. Largely because we live under the redwoods, everything ends up breeding lots of mold and spores, and even though Peg had hired her housekeeper to scour the place for me, I was worried. It's such a drafty old house, rust red, a hundred years old, with three stories. We're on the bottom floor, and you have to climb up fifty stone steps to get to it. It's beautiful, everything is green when you look out any of the windows, and there's a creek in the front yard. Deer come through the yard nearly every day, and you hear a million birds, and butterflies fly by, but my apartment is really funky. It's got one big long living room with massive built-in bookcases everywhere, and then a smallish kitchen, and then a tiny little bedroom with an elevated platform for the mattress and about five square feet of floor. Through its windows you see so much green beauty that you don't mind how cramped it is. There are little holes and gaps everywhere, and lots of spiders. Of course, there was also the kitty, who I thought might be a problem. She has been so spoiled for the last five years, like some terrible feline Leona

Helmsley, that I felt sure she would sneak into Sam's crib late at night and put a little pillow over his face or at the very least suck his milky breath out of him, like in the old wives' tales.

Sam had a slight fever following his circumcision, and his pediatrician at Mount Zion had made me promise to take the baby's temperature when I got home to make sure the fever was going down. I was scared that there would be terrible complications from the circumcision and that I had, after all, made the wrong decision and now he would get a brain fever and need emergency surgery on his wienie. Although about half of my family and friends had made circumcision seem about as humane as nipple piercing, it had been a relatively easy decision to make at the time. To begin with, I had read that penile cancer occurs almost exclusively in uncircumcised males, that uncircumcised men have much more frequent urinary tract infections, and that their female lovers have a much higher rate of cervical cancer. So there were those medical reasons, but there was also the matter of keeping the damn thing clean—you would have to cleanse the foreskin daily with, one supposes, Q-tips and 409. Who's got the time? One of my best friends had had her baby circumcised ten years ago against much protest from her family. It then turned out that her son was terribly uncoordinated as a young boy. She told me that circumcision was the best decision she ever made: "I had a terrible time teaching him to wash his *hands,*" she said.

Then there was the matter of aesthetics. I mean to cast no

24

aspersions on the presentability of anybody's wing-wang, and I certainly don't mean to imply that all uncut males look like they're from Enid, Oklahoma, but I've got to say that I prefer the look of the circumcised unit. The uncircumcised ones look sort of marsupial, or like little rodents stuck in garden hoses. And the feel of the uncut ones is a little disconcerting, with all that skin to peel back and then the worry that it won't stay, that it will swallow the missile head right back up. Women's nerves aren't bad enough as it is? So for any number of reasons, it seemed obvious to me that circumcision was a great invention—as my friend Donna put it, "It pretty much restores one's faith in Judaism, doesn't it?" And while I had not thrust my baby into the doctor's arms, urging, "Cut! Cut!," I had with a trembling bottom lip handed him over.

So there we were, me and my feverish little baby, with Pammy and Peg puttering around the house putting things away. I put Sam facedown on my lap and took off his diaper and even his little T-shirt, so he looked very sweet and vulnerable, like a chicken. Right then the kitty ran into the house and straight through the living room into the kitchen, very deliberately keeping her eyes off Sam and me. I was putting petroleum jelly on the thermometer when she tore from the kitchen, back through the living room, and out the front door, still with her eyes averted, as if she had little blinders on. A minute later, I inserted the thermometer into Sam's rectum. I think it surprised him a little bit, and right at that exact second the kitty tore back into the house and ran up to the couch to check out the new arrival. In the next few seconds, with the kitty's eyes on us, shit began spouting volcanically out of the baby's bum, and I started calling for help. The shit just poured voluminously out of Sam while the kitty looked up at me with total horror and disgust, like "You have *got* to be kidding, Annie, this one's *broken*." Like she had put her trust in me to pick one up at the pound, and this was the best I could do.

For the next few hours, she avoided him, as though the image of the shit storm were too painful and disgusting for her to forget, but by that night, she was butting her head against his and licking his ears. We all slept together on the big queen-sized futon in the living room, where it's warmer.

SEPTEMBER 16, 5:30 A.M.

We slept for six straight hours and are up nursing now. There is milk everywhere. I go around looking like I've got a wet bathing suit on under my clothes. When Sam was six days old, I took him to my little black church in Marin City, the church where I've been hanging out for four years now. I wandered in one day the year before I stopped drinking, because it was right next to the most fabulous flea market on earth, where I liked to spend time when I had terrible hangovers. I got into the habit of stopping by the church on Sundays but staying in the back, in this tense, lurky way, and leaving before the service was over because I didn't want people to touch me, or hug me, or try to make me feel better about myself. I had always pretty much believed in God, and I just naturally fell into worshiping and singing with them. Then after I got sober and started to feel okay about myself, I could stay to the end and get hugged. Now I show up and position myself near the door, and everyone *has* to give me a huge hug—it's like trying to get past the border patrol. Once I asked my priest friend, Bill Rankin, if he really believed in miracles, and he said that all I needed to do was to remember what my life used to be like and what it's like now. He said he thought I ought to change my name to Exhibit A.

Anyway, the first Sunday after Sam's birth, I kind of limped in with Peg beside me. I was holding Sam and she was holding my little inflated doughnut seat, and everyone was staring joyfully and almost brokenheartedly at us because they love us so much. I walked, like a ship about to go down, to a seat in the back. But the pastor said, Whoa, whoa, not so fast—you come up here and introduce him to his new family. So I limped up to the little communion table in the front of the half circle of folding chairs where we sit, and I turned to face everyone. The pain and joy were just overwhelming. I tried to stammer, "This is my son," but my lip was trembling, my whole face was trembling, and everyone was crying. When I'd first started coming to the church, I couldn't even stand up for half the songs because I'd be so sick from cocaine and alcohol that my head would be spinning, but these people were so confused that they'd thought I was a child of God. Now they've seen me sober for three years, and they saw me through my pregnancy. Only one (white) man in the whole congregation asked me who the father was. Toward the end of my pregnancy, people were stuffing money into my pockets, even though a lot of them live on welfare and tiny pensions. They'd sidle up to me, slip a twenty into the pocket of my sweater, and dart away.

Anyway, after I introduced Sam to them and sat down on my doughnut seat in the front row with Peg, I really got into the service. The baby was sound asleep in my arms, and I stood for the first hymn feeling very adult—an actual *mother*, for God's sake—only to discover that the doughnut seat was stuck to my bottom, and milk was absolutely pouring out of my breasts. I was not yet secure enough to hold the baby with one hand, so I was cradling him in my arms and couldn't free up either hand to pull the doughnut seat off. So I stood there bent slightly forward, warbling away, with my butt jutting out and ringed by the plastic doughnut.

• • •

But what I wanted to record today was how gorgeous, how heartbreakingly beautiful Sam's sounds are. He sounds like a baby dolphin. His breathing is so beautiful and *hard*. Pammy, who is here every day, says it's his baby Lamaze.

September 17

Sam was an angel today, no fussing, no colic, sweet and pretty as a movie baby, all eyes and thick dark hair. We went to church and a blissed-out Alma got to hold him almost the entire time. She keeps shaking her fist and saying, "This is *our* baby, *our* baby." Alma is about eighty, very very black, about four-foot-two, and wears these amazing outfits and hats that are like polyester Coco Chanels. Our pastor Harrell showed a ten-minute movie that was one of the purest statements of faith I've ever seen. It was about a tall, sweet-looking, blind man running in the Dipsea race on the arm of his best friend, who could see. The Dipsea race goes over Mount Tamalpais and ends up in the Pacific Ocean at Stinson Beach; it is grueling beyond words, very steeply uphill and then equally steeply down, exquisitely beautiful to look at, all woods and redwoods and rich rich earth and millions of wild animals. The trail lies on rugged, rocky terrain; it is hard to *hike* up and down it, let alone run. I always end up feeling like Rose Kennedy after one of those hikes, incredibly old in the joints, especially in the knees, hobbling, panting, out of it. This movie tracks the two men amid the several thousand people who run the race every year, serious runners and *King of Hearts* types together, as they leave downtown Mill Valley and head up the steps that lead to the mountain path. The footage shows this landscape to be almost biblically beautiful and difficult, just like real life. I have come to believe more with every passing year that despite technological evidence to the contrary, it is still secretly an Old Testament world out there.

The seeing man called out every root, every rock, holding the hand of his blind friend. They ran together joyfully, the seeing man calling, "Step, step, step, step, step," as they went up and down eighty-degree steps and "Roots roots roots," as they navigated trails laced with huge tree roots. They ran bobbingly, like football players stepping quickly in and out of tires during practice. "Good good, uh-oh *rock*," the seeing man would say. They both tripped a bunch of times, and the blind guy fell once, but mostly they seemed connected and safe.

I know it is odd to a lot of people that I am religious—I mean, it's odd to *me* that I'm religious, I never meant to be. I don't quite know how it happened: I think that at some point, a long time ago, I made a decision to believe, and then every step of the way, even through the worst of it, the two years my dad was sick with brain cancer, the last few years of my drinking, I could feel the presence of something I could turn to, something that would keep me company, give me courage, be there with me, like the seeing man in this movie. The movie so exactly captured how I feel these days, that Jesus is there with us everyplace Sam and I go.

When people used to say shit like this to me, I'd look at them politely and think, Well, isn't that special. Did we take our meds this morning? It was no different for me than listening to Scientologists babble about engrams and the space opera and having gotten cleared that morning. So I don't quite know what to say. Still, when I feel like I'm coming apart like a two-dollar watch, it helps me beyond words to look at myself through the eyes of Mary, totally adoring and gentle, instead of through the critical eyes of the men at the Belvedere Tennis Club, which is how I've looked at myself nearly all my life.

I don't think the men at the Belvedere Tennis Club would look at this big exhausted weepy baggy mentally ill cellulite unit we call Annie Lamott and see a beautiful precious heroic child. But Mary does.

I think that right now even Jesus and Mary are looking at each other and shaking their heads with a sort of disgusted wonder at my deterioration. (I keep trying to remember the seeing guy saying, "Roots roots roots." Being a mother is like having to navigate across a field covered with old car tires.) I was just hating Sam there for a while. I'm so goddamn fucking tired, so burnt beyond recognition that I didn't know how I was going to get through to the morning. The baby was really colicky, kvetching, farting, weeping, and I couldn't get him back to sleep. Then the *kitty* starts in, choking like mad and barfing for a while and continuing to make retching sounds for a while longer, but curiously enough it all seemed to soothe Sam, who fell back to sleep.

Much Later

Yet another Sam, not the beautiful one-armed Sam and not my Sam, but Sam the nine-year-old son of my friends Bill and Emmy, who live just down the street, came by today with his mom, and a copy of *Green Eggs and Ham* for the baby. Big Sam lay on his stomach on the floor while Emmy walked my colicky baby and I lay there on the futon being teary and ragged but also unbelievably hospitable, like Julie Nixon coming off a bad three-day Methedrine run. Big Sam was drawing a picture of dolphins and whales and an octopus for baby Sam; then he looked up from his drawing and said, "Annie, I'd like to give you some advice. Start the baby off on fruits and vegetables. I'd hold off for a while on the protein." As the morning progressed, he kept saying these odd nine-year-old boy things that really indicated how edgy he felt about old women. He must have made ten references to creepy things old women might conceivably do or that one should always be on the watch for. Finally Emmy confided to me that he had felt that way lately ever since reading "Hansel and Gretel."

My friend Armistead called the other day. I said to Sam, so that Armistead could hear, "It's your Uncle Armistead. I'm afraid he's a bit of a homo." He keeps testing negative somehow, but at least a third of his friends are dying of AIDS or are already dead. He said that when someone asks him how so-and-so is doing, he has to run through the Rolodex in his head to see if the guy is even still alive.

What a scary, savage world Sam is going to—God willing—grow up in. I don't know what I was thinking. This country is becoming a police state and six million American children go to bed hungry every night. I lay both things directly at the feet of the Republicans.

Maybe Sam will grow up and be one of the people who can turn some of this stuff around. I will raise him to be the leader of the rebel forces.

Pammy came by for tea this afternoon as she does almost every single day. We decided that giving Sam sponge baths makes him seem too much like an outpatient, so he had his first real bath today. He took it like a man. We still dress him almost exclusively in these baby bags, one-piece legless outfits with little rip cords at the bottom. It feels good to say "we," even if that means me and my best friend, instead of me and a man. I could not have gone through with this, could not be doing it now, without Pammy. In the early evenings she returns to her husband, whom she adores, but she says she counts the time until she can be with Sam again. I'm never ready for her to leave. She's my partner. In twenty-five years of friendship we've never even kissed on the lips, but in certain ways it feels like she's my lover and she's helping me raise my baby.

After Pammy went home, Sam and I played with his key chain for a long time, and it seemed to mesmerize him. He fell asleep and I finally got to eat a Häagen-Dazs bar with toasted almonds that Emmy and Big Sam had brought me earlier in the day. It made me feel that I was on the road to some small sense of normalcy. Then I broke every rule in the book by picking him up when he was sound asleep so that I could rock him in the rocking chair, holding him and smelling his clean hair and skin. I could not take my eyes off him. He didn't wake.

His key chain is made of five big plastic keys on a cord with a heart-shaped key ring. I hold up each color key for him to study, and I always say the exact same thing: "The blue one is the key to the sky, the green one is the key to the lawn, the yellow one is the key to the mustard, the red one is the key to the car, and the pink one is the key to my heart."

SEPTEMBER 19

Sam's three-week birthday is today. There's a big party scheduled for this afternoon, with Pammy, my brother Steve, Julie, who lives in the apartment upstairs, Sam, the kitty, and me. I'm sure a fabulous time will be had by all.

Sam's so beautiful and I feel such a desperate love and protectiveness that my chest tightens with it.

People kept trying to prepare me for how soft and mushy my stomach would be after I gave birth, but I secretly thought, Not this old buckerina. I think most people undergoing chemo secretly believe they won't lose their hair.

Oh, but my stomach, she is like a waterbed covered with

flannel now. When I lie on my side in bed, my stomach lies politely beside me, like a puppy.

We watched Mr. Rogers this morning. He was in an ebullient mood. When he was changing from his street shoes into his sneakers, he tossed the first one into the air with a much wilder sort of jauntiness than usual, and then caught it, and then acted so pleased with himself that he actually looked crazy. Pammy says he must have gotten laid.

Sam and I sit around and stare at each other. I call it putting on the Sam channel. I talk to him constantly—I say, "A bunch of bigheads are coming over this afternoon to celebrate your birthday," and he looks up into my face like maybe my freckles are forming themselves into familiar letters.

He's so fine all day, so alert and beautiful and good, and then the colic kicks in. I'm okay for the first hour, more or less, not happy about things but basically okay, and then I start to lose it as the colic continues. I end up incredibly frustrated and sad and angry. I have had some terrible visions lately, like of holding him by the ankle and whacking him against the wall, the way you "cure" an octopus on the dock. I have gone so far as to ask him if he wants me to go get the stick with the nails, which is what my friend Kerry says to her dogs when they are being especially bad. I have never hurt him and don't believe

I will, but I have had to leave the room he was in, go some-where else, and just breathe for a while, or cry, clenching and unclenching my fists. I have four friends who had babies right around the time I did, all very eccentric and powerful women, and I do not believe that any of them are having these awful thoughts. Of course, I know they're not all being Donna Reed either, but one of the worst things about being a parent, for me, is the self-discovery, the being face to face with one's secret insanity and brokenness and rage. Someone without children, who thinks of me as being deeply spiritual, said the other day that motherhood gave me the opportunity to dance with my feelings of inadequacy and anger, and my automatic response was to think, Oh, go fuck yourself, you New-Age Cosmica Rama dingdong head—go dance with *that* one.

I have always known, or at least believed, that way down deep, way past being kind and religious and trying to take care of everyone, I was seething. Now it's close to the surface. I feel it race from my center up into my arms and down into my hands, and it scares the shit out of me.

I hope that somehow I am and will be a wonderful mother for Sam. Perhaps I should stop asking him about the stick with the nails. I want him to grow up to have a lot of faith and to be a very gentle person, and also to be militantly on his own side, as I have come to be. I hope he grows up to be caring and amused and political, someone who does not give up on the ideals of peace and justice and mercy for everyone. Of course, on the other hand I am already actively and consciously poisoning his mind against the Republicans.

He has the most beautiful hair, his dad's hair; I feel about this like the oldest women at my church who cry out, "THANK ya, Jesus, THANK ya." I grew up feeling like E.T. with an Afro. It was too hard having this crazy hair. I still don't think I look like a white person—I look like a very pale person of color.

Sam's father has white-people's hair. He is very tall and nice-looking, although his character is a bit of a problem, in that he doesn't seem to have a great deal of it. This is probably not true—I think maybe I'm a little angry. Sometimes it feels awful, the fact that he has so entirely rejected both of us. We were friends. We slept together several times a week for several months. We talked on the phone four and five times a day, every single day. I was finishing up my book, the one that will be out in another month. We spent Christmas Eve together, Christmas morning. He gave me, ironically, a wonderful extra-large white T-shirt that has an airbrushed mama cow nuzzling her baby on it. Then two days later I found out I was pregnant, and we never spoke in a friendly way again. I don't really get it, how he can know that there is a child of his in the world and yet have absolutely nothing to do with him. Peg keeps reminding me of something that her alkie pals over in AA like to go around saying—more will be revealed.

He was so furious when I even considered keeping the baby that he temporarily lost his mind. He was calling six and seven times a day to tell me what a piece of shit I was, how unethical it was of me—and how I actually *couldn't* have the baby because he had supported Planned Parenthood all these years (which, the more I think about it, probably means that he had delivered dozens of girlfriends there for abortions). So for three or four days I was completely on the ward, just devastated, having decided that I couldn't survive any more abortions, having decided that I did in fact want this baby, and at the same time feeling it was impossible to have a baby when the father (who is six-foot-four and two hundred pounds) was so frantically and maybe violently opposed.

So I wrote down all my fears, and as I folded up the piece of paper, I said to God, "Look, I am trying to keep my sticky little fingers off the controls here; I am willing to have the baby if that is your will, if that is the right thing for us, and I am willing to have an abortion, if that would be best for the baby and me; so I am putting this in your in-box, and I'm just going to wait for my next operating instructions."

Then Sam's dad's best friend, Manning, appeared on my doorstep, and I thought he was here to browbeat me into the abortion—they've been best friends for twenty-five years (both are in their early fifties). He asked how I was doing, and I said terribly depressed, and he said, *"Why?* This is a great blessing!"* What a gutsy thing for him to do. Then we drove around on his motorcycle for a while, me with this tiny pollywog in my belly.

For two weeks I vacillated between thinking I had no choice but to have the abortion, and thinking maybe there was a way for me to pull this whole thing off and that maybe God had something up his sleeve and I was going to come into some money or something. And two weeks after I found out I was pregnant, I went to bed with so much pain in my chest that I lay there breathing like a three-hundred-pound asthmatic, just lost in the ozone, wheezing, blinking back tears. Early that morning I dreamed that I was walking along the dock of the houseboat where I used to live, carrying my little baby boy, and I tripped, and he ended up falling into the bay, and I dove in but knew I had lost him. I kept swimming downward and downward, and I kept managing to just touch his body as it fell through the really freezing black water. Then I couldn't see him at all. Through a small miracle I felt my fingers on his body again, and I actually dug them into his flesh, like the psychic surgeons supposedly do, and my fingers went all the way into him, like he was the Pillsbury Doughboy, and I got hold of him and swam to the surface. When I broke through, holding him above my head like the Olympic flame, there were friends waiting there who rushed him to the hospital, and I knew he was okay.

I woke up from the dream smiling, shook my head with

amazement, and said to myself, "Honey? Look's like we're going to have a baby."

Genewise, I could have done a lot worse. The one thing of mine that I hope Sam gets is my vision. I see like a hawk. It's sort of a joke in my family. I could always find things people had dropped in the dirt. When we were children, my father used to take us to Duxbury Reef in Bolinas on the weekends, and we'd scour the beach for bits of fossilized whalebone, which look like small pebbles with a thousand tiny bright chambers, like a bee's eyes. You'd find them mixed in with all the regular pebbles and agates and soft smooth pretty bits of old glass. I could find so many pebbles of whalebone, at least a dozen on any given outing. My dad would always shake his head and say admiringly, "Baby, you have got eyes like a hawk."

SEPTEMBER 20

I cut Sam's finger this morning while trimming his fingernails. He wept and bled, and I felt awful and went to get him a Band-Aid. There were three new tins of them, because of a particular session I'd had with my therapist when I was about six months pregnant.

I'd gone in and found myself staring for the first time at her sand tray. It really is a tray of sand, on a stand, and beside it is a bookshelf with thousands of little figurines all lined up, everything imaginable: blown-glass kitties and dogs and birds, little matchbox cars, plastic palm trees, dollhouse things, a cocktail parasol, little religious symbols and people, Jesus and Mary and Shiva and the Buddha, a long rubber snake, lots more. What you do is stand there in front of the bookshelves, look at each figure, and take down those that call out to you somehow. You put them all in a little Easter basket, and take them to the sand tray, and arrange them in little scenes according to some mysterious right-brain processing. Then you tell your therapist what is going on in the scene and why each little icon is meaningful for you.

Now, this is very scary stuff for a cerebral type, because it takes you to places you couldn't get to on your own—it rolfs old body memories out of you. I mean, who needs it, right? It's so much easier and more comfortable to stay at one's current level of mental illness. But on that particular day, I was given the willingness to work, and the desire to have some breakthroughs on Sam's behalf so that he would have a model of what it means to be whole, to be really alive and present and capable of deep, healthy, abiding love.

I've been going to this therapist, Rita, ever since I got sober, mostly because I had so many variations on the theme of low self-esteem, with conceitedness marbled in, the classic egomaniac with an inferiority complex. Or as Peg once put it, the piece of shit around which the world revolves. A couple of years ago Rita set the sand tray up in her office and explained how it worked, and for a long time I'd walk in, glance at it, and say, "I don't want to do it today," and she'd say, "That's fine," and I'd say, "Won't be doing it today," and she'd say, "Whatever." And then finally, as I said, on this one afternoon not long before Sam was born, I walked in and looked over at it and said, "Well, I guess I'll give it a shot today." And she said, "Okay, good, that's fine."

I took down six or seven figures—a cross right off the bat, because I figured a lot of dark family-secret stuff would be coming up, and the cross reminds me to stay in the light, to walk in it and tell the truth. Then I picked out a daddy, a little girl, and some kitschy stuff from Japantown like a little ceramic bridge and teeny geisha dolls. My dad was born and raised in Tokyo by Christian missionaries (he was a lifelong atheist—sometimes these things, like alcoholism, skip a generation). I grew up with a lot of little Japanese artifacts and paintings around, not to mention a psychologically abused father. I also selected a tiny box of Band-Aids like you'd buy for a little kid who has a dollhouse; it was the size of a lima bean, and I included it in my scene.

Rita asked, "Do you know why the Band-Aids are so

important to you? And why, after two years of viewing the sand tray as if it might be about to blow us both up, you include them in your first go?"

By then my throat was so constricted that I couldn't talk, and I couldn't quite figure out why until I remembered that Dad gave Mom a small and certain amount of money every month for groceries and household expenses. Because there was none extra, she couldn't blow a couple of bucks on Band-Aids, especially since little kids love them so much and use them at every opportunity, like to accessorize. So when I was small, and got a cut or scraped knee or stubbed toe, and went to get a Band-Aid, there'd often be only those little tiny ones that are almost big enough to bandage a bee. It was one of the small things that made me grow up feeling scared, like I wasn't being protected very well and I better not fall.

I realized during that session that I wanted Sam to grow up with the sense that it's safe to fall, that there's enough of the important stuff in the world for him, including Band-Aids. I still secretly worry that there isn't enough love, or money, or acclaim, and I have to do all I can to make sure I get my fair share. I'm not even sure there's really enough God to go around. I worry that people, even friends, are sucking up my portion of fame, or God, or money, the way I used to snort up cocaine like an anteater, and I will be left with only the dregs, with only the shitty little baby Band-Aids. It's so nuts, because my faith tells me the exact opposite, and my life, especially in the last ten years, has been one of great abundance and (possibly too much) attention. But anyway, after that session, I went straight to a drugstore and bought three economy-sized tins of Band-Aids.

The long and the short of it is that when I cut Sam's finger today, I thought, "Aha! Finally after thirty-five years of waiting, I can put one of those eentsy Band-Aids to work, even though we have three full tins at our disposal." But it was useless on Sam's finger; it wouldn't stick. There was no glue on the goddamn tape, and just because I'm so wasted and fragile, I got kind of weepy, because the six hundred big Band-Aids we have are too big for him. Sam watched me very intently, like his business is just to take it all in because at some point one of the bigheads is going to explain some of the rules and procedures to him.

We're going to be experiencing cash-flow problems at some point fairly soon if something unexpected doesn't come through. I saved up a bunch of money while I was pregnant, mostly by doing nonfiction pieces for various publications. Plus I get a thousand a month for a food review. Maybe we've got enough to last through the end of the year. But then, well, I don't know. I'm not too worried yet. I know God hasn't brought me this far to drop me on my head now. Plus, I mean, how bad can things get when you've got over six hundred Band-Aids? I'm sure Sam will be telling all this to a shrink someday, making me sound like a real crackpot, like some terrible cross between Squeaky Fromm and Howard Hughes in his last years, surrounded by all those boxes of Kleenex and latex gloves.

SEPTEMBER 21

My novel will be out in a few more weeks. The reviews in _Publishers Weekly_ and _Kirkus_ were both great. It all seems very far away. I can't imagine that I'll ever again have the stamina to write fiction. Writing is on my mind, though, today. It feels good to be writing this. The baby is sleeping. He was extremely hungry earlier, lunging for my breast like Ray Milland. It will be odd for him to have a writer for a parent. It was odd for me. I honestly did think that my father couldn't hold down a regular job, that that's why he worked at home at his typewriter. You'd hear him tapping away at dawn, but you could sleep through it until he woke us for breakfast. He was a wonderful storyteller. I wish I could talk to him about writing. He got sick and died right as I crossed the threshold into publication—he knew that Viking had bought my book, and he had read it and loved it. Then his brain started to get all gummed up.

I think he believed that our job, the job of a writer, is not to get up and say, "Tomorrow, in battle, most of you will die. . . ." Instead, a writer must entertain the troops the night before. I think he believed that the best way to entertain the troops is to tell stories, and the ones that they seem to like the best are ones about themselves. You can tell sweet lies or bitter truths, and both seem to help, but it's like Czeslaw Milosz said when he won the Nobel Prize for Literature, "In a room where people unanimously maintain a conspiracy of silence, one word of truth sounds like a pistol shot."

SEPTEMBER 22

The county is in the middle of a terrible heat wave. It is very hot everywhere but in this house. The baby and I both have acne. In all other ways he is unspeakably beautiful. He has the hugest, roundest eyes you can imagine, like those old Keane paintings. His hair is dark brown and thick, and he has what Pammy calls pouty baby porno lips. It's a very beautiful mouth, but all you see when you look at him are his eyes. They're not quite human; they're more like those of a gentle extraterrestrial.

· · ·

He tries to sit up and I try to help him, but he slips down like a collapsible tin camp cup.

The colic was very bad last night. Actually, it is bad almost every night now. Everyone is supportive and encouraging, but the colic still makes me feel like a shitty mother, not to mention impotent and lost and nuts. I can handle the crying for a long time, but then I feel like I'm going to fall over the precipice into total psychosis. Last night at midnight it occurred to me to leave him outside for the night, and if he survived, to bring him inside in the morning. Sort of an experiment in natural selection.

It feels like I'm baby-sitting in the Twilight Zone. I keep waiting for the parents to show up because we are out of chips and Diet Cokes. The same few people come over all the time—Pammy, my brother Steve, Emmy, Peg, my mom and Aunt Pat, and Gertrud and Rex, who are our oldest family friends. They've been like relatives for over thirty years and have been selected to be Sam's paternal grandparents (because I don't think Sam's dad ever mentioned us to his parents). Otherwise I am saying no to almost everything and everyone. This has become my specialty. My therapist, Rita, has convinced me that every time I say yes when I mean no, I am abandoning myself, and I end up feeling used or resentful or frantic. But when I say no when I mean no, it's so sane and healthy that it creates a little glade around me in which I can get the nourishment I need. Then I help and serve people from a place of real abundance and health, instead of from this martyred mentally ill position, this open space in a forest about a mile north of Chernobyl.

My brother stayed over the night before last, walked and danced with my poor gassy baby all night while I lay in the tub. Steve seems to adore being an uncle, even though the baby cries so much and has such terrible acne. Steve calls him Pizza Face.

SEPTEMBER 27

Every night between 8:30 and 12:30 Sam cries and is miserable. I have tried everything that all the baby books suggest, and it is not getting better. I feel so badly for him—I keep thinking about how hard it is for him here, especially compared to how easy and warm and floaty it was where he used to live. It's nuts. I'm so tired that I could easily go to sleep at 8:30 and sleep for twelve hours, but instead I walk the sobbing baby and think my evil thoughts—Lady Macbeth as a nanny.

Big day for Sam. He's one month old. Pammy and Steve and I celebrated by giving him another real bath in his little plastic tub, which we set up in the living room, while listening to Toots and the Maytals on the boom box. He peed all over me and into his bathwater just as the kitty walked past. She began rubbernecking with the most shocked and horrified expression on her face, clearly thinking, "Oh, my God, now I've seen *everything*." I think she had just begun to get over the trauma of witnessing the shit storm that poured out of Sam on his first day home, was just beginning to put her life back together. Steve watched Sam pee, then put his hands on his hips and said rather fiercely, "You should make him drink it."

Sam does these fabulous nipple tricks now, lolling around at my nipple, pushing it in and out of his mouth with his tongue, sort of lackadaisically, like it's a warm summer day and he doesn't have much else to do but work over his wad of chewing tobacco. And Pammy noticed a new aspect of his bath personality. He doesn't want us to think he'll ever like it, but deep down, he may be starting to.

· · ·

We were watching the news tonight while nursing, and I almost had to get up and leave the room when Bush came on. No one in the world hates George Bush as much as I do. (Who was it who said he looks like everybody's first husband?) This is a true story: I was telling Sam how I feel about Bush and why someone once referred to him as "that preppy snot in the White House," and I was saying that Sam really must grow up to be the leader of the rebel forces, and then I said to him, "Study that face for a second, listen to that whiny voice," and Sam actually looked intently at the TV for a few moments, closed his eyes, and made the loudest, most horrible fart I've ever heard. I raised my fist in the air and said, "Yes! You *got* it."

I keep wanting to do what Martin Luther King taught us—to walk in love, to love the racist and hate the racism— but I must say, it is not going very well these days. I am often beside myself with hate. I have a quote of his on the wall over my desk that says, "Let us not despair. Let us not lose faith in man and certainly not in God. We must believe that a prejudiced mind can be changed and that man, by the grace of God, can be lifted from the valley of hate to the high mountain of love." But I sometimes despair. My hatred of American conservatives apparently sustains and defines me as much as my love of Jesus does, since I don't think I'm willing to have it removed. Who would I be without it? I know I'm as much a part of the problem as anyone else and that we're all like the people in that old Dylan song who think God is on their side. Part of me does not want Sam to be like this at all, and part of me thinks that it's right and important to scorn and revile the conservatives, because—well, because they're bad, or at least they're wrong.

OCTOBER I

The worst night yet. Sam was wild with colic until midnight, and nothing helped. Nothing. I have never felt so impotent and frustrated in my life. I tried everything. I put a tape of summer night sounds complete with crickets on the boom box, because white noise is supposed to help. I put a warm hot water bottle on his tummy, held his feet, and made him do bicycle pedaling because that is supposed to help him pass gas. I surrounded him with pillows in the baby swing someone lent us, rocked and nursed and rocked and nursed, which would help for ten minutes every so often. Then the sobbing would begin again. This went on for four straight hours. I can't walk him for very long because my body is still all torn up. The wound feels like there's a fishing weight suspended from its highest point; the weight swings like a pendulum and drags the wound downward. The ache when I walk or stand up for too long is totally defeating. All I can do is try to breathe, deeply and slowly, and pray. We Christians like to go around thinking that God isn't here to take away our pain and fear but to fill it with his or her presence, and I can feel Jesus' sorrowful eyes on us as Sam and I walk and rock and nurse and listen to our white noise on the boom box, but still the frustration flushes through me again and again. If I had a baseball bat, I would smash holes in the wall.

I naively believe that self-love is 80 percent of the solution, that it helps beyond words to take yourself through the day as you would your most beloved mental-patient relative, with great humor and lots of small treats. But, God, it is so hard to feel that way today because I'm so riled up. I keep thinking of something the great black theologian Howard Thurman said, that we must try to look out at the world through quiet eyes. But I tell you, in the middle of the colic death marches, I end up looking at the baby with those hooded eyes that were in the old ads for *The Boston Strangler.*

Midnight

I felt very sorry for myself today until Peg called and reminded me of Renata Adler's wonderful line about how self-pity is maybe just sorrow in the pejorative. I wrote it down on an index card and carried it around in my pocket all day, like it was currency. The baby has fallen asleep after being just mildly colicky for a few hours, not psychotically so like last night, and the kitty is lying beside me asleep. Things are a lot better.

Steve took Sam for a while this afternoon, after dressing him in a little yellow duckling sunsuit and the Israeli cat hat that someone gave us. He looked so incredibly beautiful and tender that you almost had to look away. With a teddy bear next to the baby in the stroller, Steve figured, what woman could possibly resist? Steve is actually very handsome, six-foot-three, thin, with thick dark hair and a great nose, but he is still terribly shy and a little gangly. He trolled downtown with the baby for nearly an hour. One girl bit, but Steve didn't get her phone number. He says he is going to try again tomorrow.

4:00 A.M.

After I nursed the baby a while ago and we had gone back to sleep on the futon on the living room floor, which is still our headquarters, I heard him begin to whimper, and I thought, "Go back to sleep, you little shit." He kept whimpering, like a golden retriever whose feelings you've hurt, but he wasn't really crying, so I didn't wake up all the way. I kept shushing him and thinking, "You whiny little bugger." Finally, at least ten minutes later, with total hostility and resentment, I roused myself enough to reach over to rub his back, which sometimes helps him a little—and he wasn't there! I turned on the light, and he wasn't anywhere on the bed! I actually thought he'd been kidnapped; or *left.* It turns out he had somehow scooted off the bed and landed on the floor between the head of the futon and the wall and had just lain there whimpering. I don't think I can capture in words how I felt at that moment.

I couldn't stop thinking of a day at the end of my father's life when the brain cancer had progressed to the point where he was barely functioning. He was sometimes like an eager-to-please three-year-old, sometimes like the Rainman. He was in his early fifties. On this one day, I took him over the hill to do errands with me, and he just sat in the car totally spaced out while I ran into various stores. Everything was going okay except that it was so sad to see him in that kind of shape. Still, he was actually sort of cheerful and very very sweet. I remember we were listening to a live Pete Seeger tape. On the way home, I had to stop at the bank in Mill Valley, so I gave him a big candy bar and left him belted into the passenger seat and ran in. Of course there was a huge line, so every so often I'd run to the back of the bank and look through the window to make sure he was still there (as if someone were going to kidnap him). The last time I looked, he wasn't there—the car was empty! I felt like adrenaline had been injected directly into my heart, and I turned to stare out the windows behind the tellers, just to collect my thoughts, and through them I saw this crazy old man pass by, his face smeared with chocolate, his blue jeans hanging down in back so you could see at least two inches of his butt, like a little boy's. He was just walking on by, holding his candy bar, staring at the sky as if maybe his next operating instructions were up there.

OCTOBER 2

My mom and my Aunt Pat, my mom's twin sister, came over this morning. They are short and slightly round, originally from Liverpool, ever so slightly Monty-Pythonish, and desperately in love with the baby. Both of them work, but they come over every chance they get, and they never stay too long. This is a greatly underrated quality. I think they see Sam as royalty and me as his governess. Pat's grandchildren live in Canada and she doesn't get to see them nearly enough, so she now officially considers Sam *hers* because she can get her mitts on him whenever she wants. Her husband, my Uncle Millard, is one godfather. (The other is Manning, who told me it would be a great blessing for me to have the baby and who took me in for the amnio.) Millard is tall and skinny and hilarious and Jewish and says that my people do not know anything about educating children, so he

56

will handle things every step of the way. Millard makes it sound like Sam and I have only a few more weeks together before he begins his study of Hebrew at some yeshiva in Los Angeles. Millard will be a great godfather. He calls the baby Third Samuel.

Mom and Pat take turns holding the baby for ten and fifteen minutes at a stretch, gazing and cooing, clucking about how much he seems to adore whichever one is holding him: "Oh, you love your Nana, don't you, you love your Nana so much." "No, no, no, come here to me, darling; oh, you love your Auntie Pat so much, don't you, honey, hmm?" I lie on the futon with my eyes closed, letting their cooing and murmurs wash over me like a cool breeze.

My mother lives about twenty minutes up the highway; Pat and Millard live on the other side of the mountain. I was raised around their four kids and the kids of my father's sister, who *also* still lives in the county. We're all still pretty much around, except for my older brother, who lives with his wife in Sacramento. I was afraid when I told Mom that I was going to have a baby that she would think, Oh God, my sluttina daughter's knocked up, what will people say? But I think it was the happiest day of her life so far. That night she called every single person she has ever known to tell them the news. Some of those people say she called with tears of joy, and I think I have only seen her cry three or four times in my whole life. She even called a lot of people I have never heard of. She all but called the papers. I don't know why I was afraid: she has been a screaming liberal her entire life. She and I have sometimes not known quite what to do with each other since she and Dad split up when I was twenty-one, but we're doing okay these days. Of course, now I have a major bargaining chip in Sam: "Do this," I say, "or you'll never see the kid again." So she makes me homemade soup. Sometimes we can't communicate well, for no particular reason except that we're mother and daughter and so different: I'm so flamboyant and confessional and eccentric, and she's so essentially English, concerned with how things look to others. But she makes me these big pots of soup, and when she leaves sometimes I cry. I remember in *Franny and Zooey,* how Franny is lying around having a break-down, starving herself, saying the Jesus prayer ten thousand times a day, trying to find something holy in the world, and Zooey finally explodes in complete exasperation, crying out to her that she should simply drink her mother's soup—that her mother's love for them consecrates it, makes it holy soup.

Sam is so much bigger every day, so much more alert. It's mind-boggling that my body knows how to churn out this milk that he is growing on. The thought of what my body would produce if my mind had anything to do with it gives me the chill. It's just too horrible to think about. It might be something frogs could spawn in, but it wouldn't be good for anything else. I've had the secret fear of all mothers that my milk is not good enough, that it is nothing more than sock water, water that socks have been soaking in, but Sam seems to be thriving even though he's a pretty skinny little guy.

I'm going to have an awards banquet for my body when all of this is over.

Once Peg said that she knew God had given her this marvelous brain but that unfortunately he had put her mind inside of it. That pretty much says it for me.

I wonder if it is normal for a mother to adore her baby so desperately and at the same time to think about choking him or throwing him down the stairs. It's incredible to be this fucking tired and yet to have to go through the several hours of colic every night. It would be awful enough to deal with if you were feeling healthy and upbeat. It's a bit much when you're feeling like total dog shit. When he woke me up at 4:00 this morning to nurse, I felt like I was dying. I felt like getting up to pull down the shades and wave good-bye to all my people, but I was too tired.

He's losing his hair, but his acne is definitely better. My acne is about the same, but on the other hand, my hair isn't falling out. At least that's something. The way I'm feeling, it's a miracle that my hair isn't falling out in huge clumps and that I haven't developed a clubfoot.

There was some famous writer, I think it may have been Tolstoy, who said you must be wounded into writing but that you shouldn't write until the wound has healed. But I just want to keep typing up these notes from the middle of the hurt, although maybe they won't amount to anything.

I am definitely aware of the huge wound that having a baby makes—in addition to the fact that your ya-ya gets so torn up. Before I got pregnant with Sam, I felt there wasn't anything that could happen that would utterly destroy me. Terminal cancer would certainly be a setback, but I actually thought I could get through it. And I always felt that if something happened to Steve or Pammy, if they died, it would be over for me for a long time but that I'd somehow bounce back. In a very real sense, I felt that life could pretty much just hit me with her best shot, and if I lived, great, and if I died, well, then I could be with Dad and Jesus and not have to endure my erratic skin or George Bush any longer. But now I am fucked unto the Lord. Now there is something that could happen that I could not survive: I could lose Sam. I look down into his staggeringly lovely little face, and I can hardly breathe sometimes. He is all I have ever wanted, and my heart is so huge with love that I feel like it is about to go off. At the same time

I feel that he has completely ruined my life, because I just didn't used to care all that much.

God, they sure shit a lot, don't they? He pooped on my leg the other morning at church. Every diaper has that mustardy baby color to it. It's almost all he does. It's his *life*. Every twenty minutes, you hear him starting to go again. Pammy says he sounds like an aquarium.

We went to see Sam's doctor at Kaiser again, Dr. James, whom we love more than life itself. It turns out that my older brother, John, landscaped his garden years ago. So James likes us already because he likes his garden. You nonreligious types think, Well, that's a funny little coincidence, but we Holy Rollers say that coincidence is just God working anonymously.

I tried to get Sam to sleep all morning so he'd be in good shape for James, but it took two hours of rocking and nursing and dancing around to Joan Baez before he dropped off. I've heard that babies prefer higher tones. How did they find this out? Did they give them little questionnaires? Did they have specially trained social workers interview them in little baby-dolphin voices?

O C T O B E R 4

Have I mentioned how much I hate expressing milk? I do it nearly every day so there will be bottles of milk on hand for whoever comes by to take care of Sam, but I hate the fucking breast pump. It's the ultimate bovine humiliation, and it hurts, the suction is so strong. You feel plugged into a medieval milking machine that turns your poor little gumdrop nipples into purple slugs with the texture of rhinoceros hide. You sit there furtively pumping away, producing nebbishy little sprays on the side of the pump bottle until finally you've got half a cup of milk and nipples six inches long. It's so incredibly unsexy and secretive, definitely not something you could ever mention on "Wheel of Fortune," nothing you'd ever find in a *Cosmo* piece about ten ways to turn on your lover—crotchless underpants and a breast pump. I sit there in the kitchen miserably pumping away, feeling like Mia Farrow in *Rosemary's Baby,* pumping out a bottle of milk for the little infant Antichrist. Yesterday the refrigerator wasn't working, so after I produced a small bottle of breast milk, I had to store it in a wide-mouth thermos filled with ice, like it was a severed finger that I was about to rush to the hospital to have sewn back on. It was too ridiculous for words.

. . .

He loves rocking in the rocking chair. He loves his pacifier. I tried his pacifier myself a few days ago, sat there sucking on it while I watched TV, and then I threw it down in fear, absolutely convinced, old addict that I am, that I'd get hooked immediately. By the end of the week I'd be abusing it, lying about how often I was using it, hiding it in the hamper. . . .

Dr. James said Sam is wonderfully healthy, nine pounds, twelve ounces, twenty-one inches long, and he was like a Gerber baby on the examining table. Here I was telling James how terrible the colic was, what a difficult baby he is, and Sam was being Stevie Wonder. James said that if the colic was severe, he would prescribe a drug that has a little belladonna in it. It isn't *severe*, it's just three or four hours of kvetching every night, but I was tempted to lie to get my son some drugs. Still, I said, "No, no, I don't think so—you see, I'm an addict—it's been three years that I've been clean and sober, and I just don't feel okay about the drugs," and he said to me very patiently, very gently, "Oh, but you see, *you* wouldn't be taking the drugs—you would give them to your *baby.*"

There's a part of me that doesn't trust that I would give him the right amount. I'd give him a bit more. I have never once in my life taken the prescribed dosage. I even abuse the kitty's ear-mite medicine. If it says to spray in two little blasts, I'll spray in three. At least I don't use it on myself—yet.

OCTOBER 5

We had another bad night. We finally slept for two hours at 7:00 A.M. What a joke. I feel like thin glass, like I might crack. I was very rough changing him at 4:00 when he wouldn't stop crying. I totally understand child abuse now. I really do. He was really sobbing and the gas pain was obviously unbearable, and I felt helpless and in a rage and so tired and fucked up that I felt I should be in a home.

I can't stop crying. I cried all night, along with the baby. Pammy came over and brought two sacks of groceries, and put clean sheets on our bed, and helped us both have a bath, and just in general talked me down as if I were on a window ledge. The exhaustion, the sleep deprivation, make me feel like I'm in the bamboo cage under cold water in *The Deer Hunter.* I don't mean to be dramatic, but this must be what it feels like to be a crack baby. It's a little like PMS on mild psychedelics.

Yesterday we took a fabulous Polaroid of Pammy and Sam. Pammy is holding him up under his arms, and he has this quintessentially alarmed but very game look on his face, as though he were some great little kid you were lowering into a seat on the Ferris wheel.

OCTOBER 6, 3:45 A.M.

He just slept for four hours in a row. It feels like a small miracle. We nursed for a long time, and I liked him so much.

Then he was very wired and couldn't go back to sleep. My vagina ached terribly. I kept trying to push his pacifier in, but his jaw was sort of gritted, the way you are when you're coming down off cocaine. I just couldn't get the pacifier in. I kept feeling like I was trying to push a bit into the mouth of a wild horse.

OCTOBER 7

You won't believe this. I tell you, I *will* be out there on Market Street wearing a sandwich board for Jesus. Because *the baby smiled*. It was his first real smile that wasn't from gas. Pammy has claimed non-gas smiles for days now, but I've always just rolled my eyes at her. Yesterday she announced that he was smiling, and I looked up derisively at the ceiling, and then I heard her cooing to him, "It'll just be our little secret."

OCTOBER 8

Real tears leave his eyes now. It is almost more than I can take. Before, he'd be sobbing but there were no tears. Now there are. It seems an unfair advantage. Between the tears and the cooing and his crazy drunken-old-man smiles, it's almost unbearable. There's so much joy and pain and love and wonder in my chest and behind my eyes that it's like *The Unbearable Lightness of Being*. It's like Patsy Cline's voice.

The Giants got into the World Series today; the A's got in yesterday. The people in my family have been Giants fans for as long as I can remember. We hate the A's. We can't help it. I was explaining to Sam that Jose Canseco shouldn't get to play because of the obvious steroid use, that there is something really wrong with the guy, something really off, like with Ike Turner or George Bush. Sam studied my face intently, seeming to hang on my every word, all but nodding, looking at me like I was the risen Christ. I can't help it—I like that in a baby.

I just can't get over how much babies cry. I really had no idea what I was getting into. To tell you the truth, I thought it would be more like getting a cat.

· · ·

Now it's midnight. I can't believe I'm in such a good mood, because he has been screaming since 10:00 tonight. I am not speaking to him. He is on the futon having an episode. Every so often I pick him up and try to nurse him or walk him for a while until my yoni aches again, and then I put him back down on the futon. I'm annoyed with him. I don't think he's handling things very maturely.

I can't believe I have a book coming out soon. After a lifetime of thinking of myself as a writer, I simply cannot imagine how on earth that book managed to get itself written. It seems like someone else must have written it for me, someone who does not cry all the time and have six-inch nipples. I am grateful to whoever that was. I got my first hardback copy the other day and flipped through it. It looks and reads like a real, functioning person was involved, and there is no one fitting that description at this address.

I can't even get my teeth brushed some days. I found my toothbrush near the sink one afternoon with a neat stripe of toothpaste on the bristles from the night before, all ready to use.

Plus I no longer ever have any free hands. If I were going to write, I'd have to sit at my desk like Christie Nolan, with a unicorn stick on my forehead, my mother behind me pushing my head toward the keyboard so I could bang out letters with the stick. But she'd secretly be wanting to play with the baby instead, and she'd stand there feeling all bitter and resentful that my Aunt Pat was getting to hold him more than she was, and then she'd end up being really rough with my head, banging out the letters too hard, like she was hammering a stake into the ground.

Last night I found a baby-sitter named Megan, a lovely young six-foot-two woman from Kansas who took one of my writing workshops a couple of years ago. I think she is going to end up being a kind of underpaid au pair for us. I am already beginning to think of her as Sam's governess. Last night was the first time I've left him with anyone besides Pammy or relatives. Even though Megan looked very sweet and kind, by the time I had driven to downtown Mill Valley, four blocks away, I had decided that she was a hooker. By the Golden Gate Bridge, I had her pegged as a crack addict. But when I got home from my board meeting in the city, I was so profoundly relieved that Sam was still alive and wasn't covered with hickeys that I gave Megan my Toyota so she could drive home. Then I spent the rest of the evening worrying that I didn't know this person from Adam's housecat; I became convinced at one point that I would never see her again, that she and her pimp had totaled my car and left town. This morning she brought me a bouquet of flowers she had picked from her garden; she handed me the car keys and then rushed over to pick up the baby, while I stood there feeling like a complete idiot.

O C T O B E R   1 2

He is losing his hair in a perfect ring that circles his head, like the ring of Saturn. He looks like either a very young or a very *very* old Buddhist monk.

O C T O B E R   1 3

Last night I decided that it is totally nuts to believe in Christ, that it is every bit as crazy as being a Scientologist or a Jehovah's Witness. But a priest friend said solemnly, "Scientologists and Mormons and Jehovah's Witnesses are crazier than they *have* to be."

Then something truly amazing happened. A man from church showed up at our front door, smiling and waving to me and Sam, and I went to let him in. He is a white man named Gordon, fiftyish, married to our associate pastor, and after exchanging pleasantries he said, "Margaret and I wanted to do something for you and the baby. So what I want to ask is, What if a fairy appeared on your doorstep and said that he or she would do any favor for you at all, anything you wanted around the house that you felt too exhausted to do by yourself and too ashamed to ask anyone else to help you with?"

"I can't even say," I said. "It's too horrible."

But he finally convinced me to tell him, and I said it would be to clean the bathroom, and he ended up spending an hour scrubbing the bathtub and toilet and sink with Ajax and lots of hot water. I sat on the couch while he worked, watching TV, feeling vaguely guilty and nursing Sam to sleep. But it made me feel sure of Christ again, of that kind of love. This, a man scrubbing a new mother's bathtub, is what Jesus means to me. As Bill Rankin, my priest friend, once said, *spare* me the earnest Christians.

OCTOBER 14

Last night was death. Vietnam. He was colicky from 10:00 till nearly 1:00. At midnight I broke under the strain and called this organization called Pregnancy to Parenthood. They help stressed-out parents and have a twenty-four-hour switchboard that I think is to prevent child abuse. I felt humiliated calling and was crying quite hard, and Sam was crying quite hard, and I told the person on the line that I didn't think I was going to hurt him but that I didn't think I could get through the night. So the person rang the clinical director at home, spliced my call through, and we talked for over an hour. Sam eventually went to sleep. She recommended I go on a wheat-free, dairy-free diet to see if it helps. Mostly she was just there for me in the middle of the night. We talked until I was okay again. Sam woke up a few hours later and nursed peacefully.

This morning someone from North Point Press called and read the *Chronicle* review of my new book to me, the review that will run on Sunday. I had completely forgotten that today is my publication date, that I actually have a book coming out of the chute right now. Anne Tyler raved in the *Chronicle*, and the *New York Times* review reads like my mother wrote it. So that's all good news. I really can't relate, though. I keep thinking, Well, that's nice. I'm pleased and it's a huge shot in the arm—still, I keep thinking that the jig is just about up. The phone will ring and the authorities will at first gently try to get me to confess that I didn't actually write the book, and if I continue to claim that I did, they'll turn vicious, abusive: "Look at yourself! You're a goddamn mess. You've got a functioning IQ of less than 100, your nerves are shot, your hands tremble, you're covered with milk and spit-up. You have trouble writing out *checks*, yet you want us to believe you produced a novel? Well. We don't *think* so." Then they'll make me go get a job with the phone company.

Later in the day I took Sam into town in his stroller, and I felt like I was waddling. When I got home from the hospital, I had lost all but about five of the twenty-five pounds I'd gained, and nursing, like Lady Pac Man, gobbles up so many calories that I've lost a few more, but I tell you, things have not gotten higher and firmer in the last nine or so months. My butt, she is low down in the water now, Mama. I was wearing a skirt and could hear my thighs slap softly against each other as we walked along. They sounded like waves lapping the shore. I remember my friend Nora saying once that she was seriously considering suicide, but that she wanted to lose five pounds first.

The sun was pouring in through the tops of the redwoods, and the air was like velvet. Birds were singing. I heard the burbling fluty song of a mockingbird. Sam slept.

We went to the bookstore and my book was in the window and there was a huge stack of them right by the cash register, so I didn't have to do my usual routine of furtively moving them to places where more people would see them. For the first time, I've been too wasted and preoccupied to call all the big Bay Area bookstores and ask them if they have copies yet. I've always called bookstores over and over again for the first few weeks after publication, disguising my voice, either by pinching my nostrils shut or by trying to sound vaguely English. Sometimes I pretend not to know how to spell my last name. "Do you have Anne Lamott's new book?" I've always asked. "I think it's L-a-m-o-n-t. No, wait, maybe it's t-t, L-a-m-o-*t*-t." I'm sure I've never fooled anyone. I'm sure they put their hand over the mouthpiece of the phone and whisper, "It's her again" to the other clerks. I held Sam up to the window of the Book Depot so he could study the jacket of my book, and I said, "That's my book, honey. I *write*," and he looked at me with a mildly patronizing expression. You could just tell he was thinking, "Sure you do."

OCTOBER 15

Three days off wheat and milk products, two nights with no colic. I'm sure it's a fluke and that the crying will start again. He coos and gurgles.

Yesterday was day one of the World Series, S.F. against Oakland. Steve came by to watch. We had all these fabulous wheat-free, dairy-free snacks, and he and Sam lay on the couch together wearing their Giants shirts. Sam's is the size of your hand. He looks very sporting in it, very manly. The Giants got slaughtered. Steve explained all the key plays to Sam and hinted darkly that if Sam grows up to be an A's fan, he will lose his share of the vast Lamott estate. It was obvious from Sam's expressions that he didn't think much of Canseco.

He's very active all of a sudden, kicking all over the place, like Nadia Comaneci. He looks ready to walk. I hold him up so he's standing on the dressing table or floor or whatever, and I say urgently, "Lock your knees! Lock your knees, I'm going to let go!" He looks puzzled but game.

His hands are like little stars.

OCTOBER 19

Last night I crawled into bed with Sam and the kitty on the futon in the living room, with religious music on the tape player; the kitty curled up next to Sam's head, and both of them purred. After a minute I felt something under the covers with my bare foot. Whatever it was, it was big and wet. With a seven-week-old baby you just know it's gotta be something funky. I lay there not moving, thinking about the scene in *The Godfather* with the horse's head, and I slowly pushed back the covers, sort of expecting the worst because on top of everything the kitty has had such doubts about my abilities as a hunter that she's been bringing me and the baby all sorts of delicacies lately. It turned out to be a wet diaper.

OCTOBER 20

There was a huge earthquake in the Bay Area yesterday. I came in from the kitchen to check on Sam, who was sleeping and who has a cold, and suddenly the whole house was swaying and there was a low roar. Everything was shaking, and I actually thought at first that John and Julie, who live in the flat above us, were using an industrial floor waxer. Then I realized what was going on, and I looked over at where Sam lay asleep in his bassinet, right beneath the built-in bookcases, and I was immobilized. All of the big heavy books could have fallen down onto him and crushed him, and I couldn't move. Like a nightmare. It felt like it lasted about fifteen seconds, and when it was over I rushed to the bassinet and picked up the baby. He continued to sleep. Then Julie came running down to make sure we were okay, and we turned on the TV. At first there was no reception, but then finally there was a picture, and the first reports made it sound like San Francisco looked like Nagasaki, like the whole city was on fire. A section of the Bay Bridge was down, and there was total pandemonium and also immediate acts of heroism and bravery. Julie and I both voiced huge, concerned, compassionate thoughts about what was going on, feeling really awful and impotent. One small difference in our reaction was that Julie, near tears, sat staring at the set, wondering out loud if her husband was still alive, while I was rather horrified to discover that I was worried about how this would affect sales of the book. This made me feel just great about myself, as you can imagine. So did my other main concern, which was that if the World Series had to be postponed, it would completely ruin my life, and when I got up to make Julie a cup of tea, I limped to the kitchen feeling like a medieval dwarf with a lot of small broken teeth.

In the old days this feeling of loathsomeness would have lasted for days, would have triggered that old familiar fear that if people could really know me, they would discover that I make the Joan Collins character on "Dynasty" look like Helen Keller. But now I'm just too tired. I know Sam will grow up and have all these terrible secret thoughts, too. His self-centered, petty, envious, conniving mule-stupid side will haunt him; he will be plagued by terrible self-doubts and fear. I hope I can remember to tell him then that on the night of the 1989 earthquake, I was trying to figure out how distributors would be able to get copies of my book into the stores, what with the Bay Bridge down and all. I guess he'll have to figure out someday that he is supposed to have this dark side, that it is part of what it means to be human, to have the darkness just as much as the light—that in fact the dark parts make the light visible; without them, the light would disappear. But I guess he has to figure other stuff out first, like how to keep his neck from flopping all over the place and how to sit up.

Julie's husband, John, finally got home around 8:00 with reports of chaos in the city, and of course the Bay Bridge Series *has* been postponed. I am trying to be a good sport about the whole thing, but it is not going terribly well. Steve came over and ended up spending the night. We watched the news until well past midnight, and it was strangely comforting for normal life to have ceased temporarily. You knew you were going to get to sit around in front of the television set for the next few days and eat your wheat-free, dairy-free snacks. In a terrible way, it was like being in the middle of a long, lurid thriller, where no matter what else happened in your private life, you knew your plans were set for the next few days. I found that I was getting stoned on all the drama and adrenaline. It was so mesmerizing, so compelling, that I found it mood-altering, even though I couldn't really relate. I'd thought I was going to spend the next few days watching the World Series on TV. Instead I'd be watching the earthquake reports, and there was a blasé part of me that thought, Well, whatever, just as long as there's *something*.

No one I know was hurt. It's very sad, but it could have been a thousand times worse. I kept praying that everyone would be okay and stick together and take care of one another. I kept thinking of small good-guy things I could do to help, but I couldn't really concentrate because Sam had a cold. I couldn't suck out the mucus with the rubber-bulb aspirator like normal functioning mothers are supposed to be able to do, and he was obviously quite uncomfortable even though I had a humidifier going. I wanted to call 911 and say, "I'm sorry about the earthquake, but my baby's terribly congested! You must come immediately!"

· · ·

I notice I'm not so wildly surprised to find him alive every morning. In the earlier days, when I'd first hear his kvetchy little voice, I'd feel that it was proof enough that there was a God in heaven. Now when I hear him start to whimper, I feel just the merest bit testy. I try to con him into sucking on his pacifier for a while so I can sleep for a few more minutes.

The diet is definitely working. I'd say the colic is 85 percent gone. He still fusses and whines for a couple of hours every evening, but it's pretty manageable now. Steve says Sam cries just like Cheswick, the short, bald, frantic guy in *One Flew Over the Cuckoo's Nest*, who was always whining, "I don't *want* McMurphy's cigarettes, Nurse Ratched, I want *my* cigarettes . . ."

O C T O B E R   2 3

My friend Orville dropped by yesterday with a beautiful red and green satin stuffed fish from China, embroidered with all sorts of things that the presence of this fish will protect us from: scorpions, spiders, snakes. I kept trying to convey to Orville how wasted I am by the baby's needs, while the whole time Sam lay there doing his baby Jesus routine. He's so beautiful you can't take your eyes off him. But

Orville, who raised a baby son fifteen years ago, says he remembers clearly how insane things get with an infant around. He said that even with a mate, it's like having a clock radio in your room that goes off erratically every few hours, always tuned to heavy metal.

Sam sleeps for four hours at a stretch now, which is one of the main reasons I've decided to keep him. Also, he lies by himself on the bed staring and kicking and cooing for fifteen to twenty minutes at a time. I had these fears late at night when I was pregnant that I wouldn't be able to really love him, that there's something missing in me, that half the time I'd feel about him like he was a Pet Rock and half the time I'd be wishing I never had him. So there must have been some kind of a miracle.

I never ever wish I hadn't had him.

But I do sometimes wish I had a husband and a full-time nanny. And that I could still have a few drinks now and then. I am coming up on three and a half years clean and sober. The memories are still very clear of how lost and debauched and secretly sad my twenties and early thirties were, how sick and anxious I felt every morning. I thought at the time that I was having a lot of fun, except that the mornings were really pretty terrible. But there are still times when these movies start to play in my head, where I see myself putting the baby down to sleep and then sitting and sipping one big, delicious Scotch on the rocks. Just sipping, just sipping one fucking drink. Is that so goddamn much to ask? I just want that kind of relief, that smoothing of the sharp edges. The only fly in the ointment is that if I went to a liquor store and put some money on the counter for a bottle of good whiskey, I might as well put Sam on the counter, too, because I know I will lose him if I start drinking again. I know I would lose every single thing in my life that is of any real value. I couldn't take decent care of *cats* when I was drinking. They'd run off or get hit by cars or get stolen, because I'd forget to leave windows open for them or wouldn't come home for a couple of nights in a row. So I don't know, I guess I won't have a drink today. Maybe tomorrow, *probably* tomorrow, but not today.

Sam has this great roar now, like maybe he's about to cry, but then it turns out that he just feels like roaring because that's the kind of guy he is—he's a roaring kind of guy—and because he's coming into his own, like "I am baby, hear me roar, in numbers too big to ignore. . . ." Then he burns his diaper.

Half the time I'm completely winging this motherhood business. I get so afraid because we are running out of money. We have enough to live on for maybe two more months. Also, I just had no idea I had so much rage trapped inside me. I've never had a temper before. I've always been able to be mellow or make jokes. But we went through a difficult patch this evening when Sam was being hard to please, whiny and imperious and obviously feeling very sorry for himself, and at first I could kind of roll with it, shaking my head and thinking, It's because he's a *male*, he's having an *episode*, this is very familiar stuff to me, he's already got testosterone poisoning. But I couldn't get him to stop, and it wore me down. It was one of those times when I desperately needed to be able to hand him over to someone, like, say hypothetically, a mate, and there wasn't anyone. So suddenly all this bile and old fear of men and abandonment stuff were activated in my head. All these furious thoughts about Sam's father. Sam was so exasperating that I could feel fury coursing through my system, up my arms into my hands, like charged blood. I made myself leave the room, just left him crying in his bassinet in the living room, which is what Bill Rankin said to do once before. I went to the tiny bedroom in the back, and breathed, and prayed for major help. The next thing I knew, I had decided to take him for a walk in the stroller in the dark.

It was warm and the stars were just coming out; the sky seemed unusually deep. I said to God, I really need help tonight, I need you to pull a rabbit out of your hat. One minute later Bill and Emmy and Big Sam came walking along the road toward us. So we stopped to talk for a few minutes. Big Sam is such a brilliant and gentle little guy, so artistic and tender with the baby that it helped me to breathe again. I felt completely back in the saddle by the time we all said good-bye.

Part of me loves and respects men so desperately, and part of me thinks they are so embarrassingly incompetent at life and in love. You have to teach them the very basics of emotional literacy. You have to teach them how to be there for you, and part of me feels tender toward them and gentle, and part of me is so afraid of them, afraid of any more violation. I want to clean out some of these wounds, though, with my therapist, so Sam doesn't get poisoned by all my fear and anger.

I nursed him for a long time tonight. He's so beautiful it can make me teary. I told him I was sorry for thinking such sexist stuff about his people. He listened quietly and nursed and stared up into my face. I wanted to justify it, tell him about all the brilliant but truly crummy men out there, and let's not even get *started* on the government, but then I began humming some songs for him until he fell asleep. Then it was perfectly quiet.

OCTOBER 25

He's very brilliant, this much is clear. He's learned to comfort himself without the pacifier by sucking on his hands and fists, like a lion with a bone. I wish *I* could sit in public places slobbering away on my own fist. It looks very comforting. The colic is gone. I am still wheat-and-dairy-free. Also, mostly shit-free, bullshit-free. I am finally saying no when I mean no, which is a lot of the time, especially when people want me to come to their house for a party. People have been inviting me and Sam to their parties lately, for God knows what reason. Everyone knows I don't do parties or dinners. Everyone knows I don't do "do's." It's just torture for me. "Why is that?" people have always asked, and all I can do is shrug. I think it's either that I'm not remotely well enough for that sort of thing or because I've gotten *too* well. Who knows, but I would honestly rather spend an hour getting my teeth cleaned than an hour mingling. I am absolutely serious about this. I get so nervous that I actually skulk, and then I get into this weird shuffling-lurk mode. It's very unattractive. I look like a horse who can count, pawing the ground with one hoof. I don't know why people would even bother inviting me.

But in the old days I used to get sucked in and say yes to everybody and be there for them, showing up at their parties, helping them move, or staying on the phone with them too long. I'd try to entertain or help or fix, nurse them back to health or set them straight. Now I do the counting-horse shuffle and shake my head and say I just can't do it, can't come to the party, can't do the favor, can't stay on the phone. I want Sam to understand when he grows up that "No" is a complete sentence. It's given me this tremendous sense of power. I'm a little bit drunk on it. I ended up saying no to a couple of things I really wanted to do with friends, then had to call them up and beg, "Take me back, take me back."

Also, it's great to be so taken up by Sam that I don't have to deal with men. It's like that beautiful old movie by Vittorio de Sica, *A Brief Vacation.* I have had a lot of men do stuff to me over the years, and I sanctioned it, but I did not want it. I have listened so attentively to the most boring, narcissistic men so that they would like me or need me. I'd sit there with my head cocked sweetly like the puppy on the RCA logo. On the inside I would feel like that old poem by Philip Levine, about waiting until you can feel your skin wrinkling and your hair growing long and tangling in the winds. It was like these men held me hostage. I'd think about chewing my arm off to get out of the trap so I could rush home and hang myself, but at the same time I'd need them to think well of me. Now I all but say, Oh, I'm so sorry, but I'm on this new shit-free diet. Now there's Sam, me, Uncle Jesus, Pammy, Steve, a few friends, a few relatives, and the kitty.

Sam has a Big Brother now named Brian. He has come the last two Tuesdays to take care of him for a couple of hours. He is married to my good friend Diane, who is in her mid-forties and does not want children, whereas Brian is ten years younger and adores them. He signed on to be a Big Brother in Marin last year and got assigned a kid who thought he was a total dork and who was ashamed of Brian's big land-boat Buick. They just couldn't connect at all. So when I was about to deliver, Diane came to me and asked if Brian could be Sam's formal and official Big Brother. Brian's another sober alcoholic, very kind and funny. It's been wonderful. He's already learned to change diapers and feed Sam bottles of pre-pumped breast milk and bathe him, and he puts him in the Snugli or the stroller and takes him to the park down the street. They discuss guy stuff. Brian gets tears in his eyes when he talks about Sam because he is so grateful and surprised that they get to have each other. I sense that they will be together for life.

There are great men in Sam's life, the best men the world produces. It's another kind of miracle, that he has this devotion, that we both do, but still it will probably hurt beyond words someday that he doesn't have his dad in his life. I'm just going to have to tell him that not everybody has a father. Look at me, I will tell him: I don't have a father, and I don't have a swimming pool, either. But Sam will have a tribe. You can't help but believe that these other men will help Sam not have such a huge sense of loss. They'll be his psychic Secret Service.

Our best family friends, Rex and Dudu, are perfect grandparents for Sam. They have been my parents' best friends since my older brother John was a baby, before I was born. They lived half a mile away from us when we were growing up, and I

always thought of them as our godparents, although they were
called our aunt and uncle. Dudu's real name is Gertrud;
"Dudu" is what she called herself when she was a tiny girl in
Germany. We've never called her anything else, and people
have always looked at us strangely if we mention her, like we
might also have an Uncle Piles and a cousin Weewee. But to
me it is one of the most beautiful names I know because she
has been a saint to my family. Rex fell in love with her after
the war ended and brought her to America. I think there was
a lot of prejudice against her when she first came to live here.
They have a daughter who lives in Oregon, and a son who lives
in L.A., and neither one intends to have children. Dudu and
Rex, like my father and my mother, were born to be grandparents. They are in their early seventies now, both of them
gorgeous and fit. They still spend about a third of their time
in the mountains, mostly at Yosemite, hiking and backpacking
and skiing. I cannot keep up with them. I always end up
lagging way behind, feeling like a person who is crawling over
the sand toward a mirage, while they bound ahead pointing
out wildflowers. They love John and Steve and me exactly as
though we were their own children, and we love them like they
are our other set of parents. They stayed with us around the
clock at the cabin when my dad was dying, helped us keep him
clean and okay those last few days, helped us take care of him.
I know the whole thing broke their hearts. I don't think you
can ever really get over the death of the few people who matter

most to you. It's too big. Oh, you do, the badly broken leg does heal, and you walk again, but always with a limp.

I asked them to be Sam's paternal grandparents when I was two months pregnant. I said then that it would need to be *very* formal and official; they would have to be actual blood grandparents, buying him expensive holiday outfits and taking him to Disneyland when he was old enough. They were overjoyed. Since he was born, they have been blown away with love for their baby grandson. Just blown away. Mom and Dudu compare grandmother notes every other day. I have been taking Sam over to their house the last few Wednesday nights so I can go to the movies with friends. It is just great to get away from Sam. At first. At first it makes me feel like Zorba the Greek. But then the jungle drums start beating and I feel like you do when you're having a massive nicotine craving. This week, I sat alone in a theater watching this totally dumb movie, this warm perfumed poopoo, but happily overeating in the dark, totally happy to be away from Sam, for about twenty minutes. Then the longing to be with him again became so intense that I sat there hyperventilating. There was a ten-minute patch of time when I must have looked like I was doing Lamaze. I felt like I was totally decompensating. I finally had to leave, get an ice cream, and walk around town for a few minutes. The theater is not very far from where Rex and Dudu live. They have lived in the same home for forty years, in the town where I grew up. I killed as much time as was humanly possible, which turned out to be about an hour and a half, and then I drove up the hill to their house. They were sitting on the couch, side by side, Sam was in Rex's arms, drinking his bottle, and Rex and Dudu both looked stoned. I've noticed this when I pick Sam up at my mother's, too, when she and my Aunt Pat have taken him for a while. I always find them sitting side by side on the couch, sometimes with my Uncle Millard, taking turns holding the baby, giving him his bottle, cooing at him, looking stoned. All the older relatives, and in fact Pammy, too, end up looking like Woody Allen in *Sleeper* when he's dressed up as the robot butler, and has taken way too many hits off the futuristic drug called the Orb, and is sitting slumped against the wall, clutching the Orb romantically to his chest, looking like he's about to pass out.

I sent my agent a picture of me holding Sam in my lap, and she wrote back, "Your hands have become the hands of a mother."

Did I ever tell you about the day I was trying to make rice water, which is an old home cure for colic? You just boil rice in a lot of water and then strain the water off and put it in a bottle. But I was so wasted with exhaustion that I wasn't vigilant enough, and the water kept getting absorbed and I'd end up with a huge pot of cooked rice, nice wet cooked rice and not one drop of rice water. So I'd try again, and the exact same thing would happen. Luckily Steve dropped by. He ate three or four massive bowls of the rice, with butter and teriyaki sauce. I never did get that rice water made.

OCTOBER 26

Sam's forgotten how to suck on his hands. Now he just sort of licks them as they spastically pass by.

I gave Pammy the little baby bags with the rip cords at the bottom that Sam wore almost exclusively the first month, because she and her husband are planning to adopt a baby next year. Sam is her training baby. He needs things with legs in them, now that he's a kicking guy. Pammy and I both got all teary. I felt like my son had become a man. Soon we'll be having fights about the car, and he'll say hurtful things about the music I like.

I think "Sam" was really the right name for him. You see all these kids running around these days named Sterling and Carleton, and they already look like little Sterlings and Carletons in their little Kennebunkport clothes.

OCTOBER 28

I got to talk to my therapist on
the phone for half an hour today. All I wanted to do all day
was eat—assault-eat, as someone put it. I can just barely
tolerate the feelings I have on bad days. And Rita said that was
fine, to stuff it down, if it gave me relief. There's just one real
fly in the ointment, though: after chowing down I feel even
worse, full of remorse, fearful, stunned, and big as a house.
Rita said, "The awful news is that you probably just have to
go ahead and feel the feelings and grieve the grief." I said, "I
hate that shit. I'm not going to call you anymore." I could hear
her smiling over the phone. I started to laugh, too, and then
I started to cry. Rita said we should probably hang up so I
could really let go and cry, and I did, just sobbed while the
baby slept, and when I was done, it was like coming out of a
trance, and I didn't feel like eating anymore. . . . Well, maybe
just a little.

Luckily, Peg brought over the most amazing Chinese
chicken salad for dinner, and a six-pack of Diet Cokes. She
danced with Sam to Hoagy Carmichael while I took a long,
hot bath. She and I used to do huge quantities of cocaine in
North Beach, big oat bags of coke, but not share any with each
other, just slip off to the bathroom with our vials alone, then
meet at the bar, hammered out of our minds, waiting for each

other to finish talking so it would be our turn to talk again. We were the personifications of that Fran Lebowitz line: there's talking and there's waiting. Both of our dads died of brain diseases after long lingering illnesses, hers of Alzheimer's and mine of cancer, and after we'd had hundreds of drinks, we'd get into the big boo-hoo. She was a worse cokehead than I was, only because she had more money. I did a lot more Methedrine, because it was cheaper. Also, she drank in the morning, which I tried very hard not to do. She'd swill down a couple of shots first thing, just to get all the flies going in one direction, and I used to think, Boy, she's *really* got a problem.

O CTOBER 2 9

He's two months old today, quiet and happy and alert. Pammy is coming for a pool party this afternoon. Actually, we're just going to give him a bath and then take turns holding him while we watch TV. Maybe it's not much of a life, but it's our life. It's all so absolutely amazing. I don't remember what Pammy and I used to talk about before that day, December 27 of last year, when I walked into the bathroom to find the results of an at-home pregnancy test and gasped out loud, there in the doorway, frozen for a while, just another woman staring fixedly at a blue-tipped stick.

OCTOBER 30

Emmy and Bill came by with some groceries. Big Sam asked with real concern, "Have you ever noticed how similar French and English are? Like 'le drugstore'? 'Le week-end'? 'Le hot dog'?"

OCTOBER 31

We walked into town late this afternoon with Pammy, and it was strangely thrilling to see how many adults got dressed up for Halloween. It was touching to see all these people who usually walk around in carefully constructed disguises, doing very impressive impersonations of busy adults, but who on the inside are secretly divas and pirates, clowns and heroes. All the stuff in their heads found its way out onto the streets today—in the market, the banks, the drugstore. There were whiskers, glitter, slapshoes, blood. My head swam with wonderful memories of treasure hoarding and gluttony. The best thing is that you really feel that fall is here. There's a tang in the air.

Sam was very funny all afternoon, so dignified and serious. "Dignity is very important, my darling," I told him. "Second only to kindness." He is so focused and attentive that one expects him to nod gravely. He struggles to get his thumb into his mouth, but it's as though his arms were in a zero-gravity atmosphere of their own; they go flying through his field of vision like unsecured things in a spaceship.

Megan took him to the park for a couple of hours today, and I got a little bit of work done, taking some notes for a novel, getting down some of the raw material. I don't know if anything will come of it, but this is always how my novels start. A few small visions, and then the story and themes begin to emerge, like a Polaroid developing. We are slowly running out of money. I am just going to try to stay faithful and get my work done.

My breasts were bursting with milk by the time Megan and the baby returned. Sam nursed for forty-five minutes, like he was at his own private keg party, then belched and passed out.

"Do you mind if I tell people you're his governess instead of his baby-sitter?" I asked Megan.

"Of course not," she said.

"Wouldn't you think having a governess would almost make up for his not having a father?" I asked.

"Yes, I would," she said. We sat for a moment in silence.

"Can you teach the child French?" I asked.

"I can try," she said.

Megan is very kind and exquisitely competent and laughs at all my jokes. Today we compared notes on how hard it was to be such strange sizes in seventh grade. She was nearly six feet tall already—now she is six-foot-two—and I was about four-foot-two. I heard this woman speak a couple of years ago who talked about our bodies being our little earth suits, and I asked Megan if she thought it would have made any difference if we'd been able to think that way at thirteen. She didn't know. But it helped me to talk about earth suits out loud because I hadn't thought of them in a while. It's so easy to be mean to yourself when you're fat and your thighs continue moving after you've come to a stop.

I'm trying to be extremely gentle and forgiving with myself today, having decided while I nursed Sam at dawn this morning that I'm probably just as good a mother as the next repressed, obsessive-compulsive paranoiac.

I think we're all pretty crazy on this bus. I'm not sure I know *anyone* who's got all the dots on his or her dice.

But once an old woman at my church said the secret is that God loves us *exactly* the way we are *and* that he loves us too much to let us stay like this, and I'm just trying to trust that.

NOVEMBER 1

Sam sort of played with a rattle today, but he kept whacking himself in the eye. He has huge round saucer eyes. They make me remember a Pauline Kael review years ago where she referred to someone's eyes as big blue headlights. Megan suggested that I should get Sam little grates to cover them so that things don't fall in.

Yesterday I didn't have enough milk. I nursed him at 10:00 in the morning, and there wasn't enough, he was crying for more. Julie from upstairs suggested we try a can of soy formula, and he guzzled it down like John Belushi. So I panicked and decided that all these weeks he's been starving to death on my sock-watery milk and that his body has had to cannibalize itself for him to stay alive. Plus, he's had another head cold recently, and of course the logical conclusion yesterday was that he is a sickly baby. Also, an addict: I've been giving him

Robitussin as per the Kaiser nurse's instructions, and he *really* likes it. I felt that if he could talk, he'd be saying, "Oops, oops, time for more," even if it had only been an hour or so and that soon he would start lying in order to get it: "No, that wasn't me you gave it to," he'd say, "that was another baby."

The La Leche League—they are breast-feeding specialists—saved the day yet again. They said simply to drink tons of fluids and nurse as often as possible, and today I'm a glorious Florentine fountain of milk, standing like a birdbath in the garden with milk spouting forth from every orifice.

I'm learning to call people all the time and ask for help, which is about the hardest thing I can think of doing. I'm always suggesting that other people do it, but it really is awful at first. I tell my writing students to get into the habit of calling one another, because writing is such a lonely, scary business, and if you're not careful you can trip off into this Edgar Allan Poe feeling of otherness. It turns out that motherhood is much the same. I'm beginning to believe what I always tell my students, which is that someone, somewhere, is always well if you're just willing to make enough phone calls.

He lies on his back for long stretches now, totally alert and totally spaced out at the same time, like he's on acid or in the presence of God.

. . .

Last night he slept from 9:00 till 2:00, and we nursed for a while, and then he slept again until 6:30. He wakes up joyful and ready to go. Somehow he has gotten it into his head that we are busy, active people and need to get up early. I lie there nursing him with sand in my eyes, looking and feeling like a snake halfway through shedding her first skin.

Yesterday Mom and Aunt Pat took care of him for a few hours, and Mom asked how much he weighed. I didn't know. So Sam and I got on Mom's scale together, and when the scale weighed 149, I felt on the verge of hysterics because at Kaiser a week earlier I had only weighed 137. My mom said, really nicely, "But, honey, you're still holding the *baby*," which absolutely had not crossed my mind. I said, almost crying, "Mommy, I'm so tired."

I wish I could get away with one or two glasses of wine or half a Valium, or even with getting to eat my body weight in Mexican food and chocolate every couple of days. I just desperately want to check out for a couple of hours now and then. I want a little relief. I have never been all that big on reality. I've had every single major disorder known to woman, from alcoholism to workaholism, anything to avoid having to feel my feelings. Everything in fact except gambling, which is probably right around the corner. Come to think of it, I've found myself getting overstimulated at the change machines in Laundromats. Sometimes I stand there compulsively putting in dollar bills, feeling a bit of a rush each time the four quarters shoot out.

If I weren't nursing, if I weren't dairy-free, I'd definitely take to bed with the Häagen-Dazs today.

NOVEMBER 3

He laughed today for the first time, when Julie from upstairs was dangling her bracelets above his head while I was changing his diaper. His laughter was like little bells. Then there was the clearest silence, a hush, before total joyous pandemonium broke out between Julie and me. Then we both stared almost heartbrokenly into his face. I thought of Wallace Stevens' "Thirteen Ways of Looking at a Blackbird," verse five:

> I do not know which to prefer,
> The beauty of inflections
> Or the beauty of innuendoes,
> The blackbird whistling
> Or just after.

NOVEMBER 4

I had a session over the phone with my therapist today. I have these secret pangs of shame about being single, like I wasn't good enough to get a husband. Rita reminded me of something I'd told her once, about the five rules of the world as arrived at by this Catholic priest named Tom Weston. The first rule, he says, is that you must not have *any*thing wrong with you or anything different. The second one is that if you do have something wrong with you, you must get over it as soon as possible. The third rule is that if you can't get over it, you must pretend that you have. The fourth rule is that if you can't even pretend that you have, you shouldn't show up. You should stay home, because it's hard for everyone else to have you around. And the fifth rule is that if you are going to insist on showing up, you should at least have the decency to feel ashamed.

So Rita and I decided that the most subversive, revolutionary thing I could do was to show up for my life and not be ashamed.

NOVEMBER 5

I got out the miniature Snickers that the little no-necks didn't get on Halloween night, and I ate at least a dozen, even though they are not wheat-or-dairy-free. Looking back, I think it was an act of rebellion, some kind of subconscious "Fuck you" to Sam. At the time I was so busy getting stoned on the sugar that I didn't stop to figure out what was going on. I just wanted not to feel everything so intensely. Every time I went to get another one, though, I'd feel that Sam was giving me the eye. "Honey," I'd say, "you gotta eat them, or they go bad. Look, they have *dates* on them." He can look very stern. The awful thing is that he was sick and colicky by dinner. It is a huge struggle tonight to treat myself like a beloved relative. I'm so sorry.

NOVEMBER 6

His arms and hands still have wills of their own. They float erratically above him, suddenly darting into his field of vision like snakes, causing him to do funny little Jack Benny double takes.

Yet at the same time, he can now hug. He really holds on when we walk or rock. And he's *very* alert, constantly sizing up the world and then babbling away in his native Latvian.

He got his DPT shot Monday, and we both cried. It was a mean trick, because he was in the best mood, kicking and making bubbles for me and Dr. James, and then some vicious, sociopathic nurse comes in and sticks needles into his leg. He was frantic. I wept and then said to the nurse, in a teary but jocular way, "Do most mothers cry the first time?" and she looked at me with puzzled condescension and said, "No."

Pammy came over this afternoon with a soft Babar rattle for him. I heard her telling him conspiratorially, "I'm the one who didn't take you in and make you get hurt." She has confessed that she thinks of me as the womb who made it possible for them to be together. She and her husband have been trying for ten years to have a baby. I don't know why I get to have Sam, but then, she gets to have her husband.

Sam cried a lot last night. I kept remembering my friend Michelle, who would go out in the field by her house and sit in a rocking chair while Dennis took care of their first baby, Katherine, who cried all the time. Michelle just sat out there in the field for hours, rocking miserably by herself, saying over and over, "This is not a good baby."

· · ·

No one ever tells you about the tedium. (A friend of mine says it's because of the *age* difference.) And no one ever tells you how crazy you'll be, how mind-numbingly wasted you'll be all the time. I had no idea. None. But just like when my brothers and I were trying to take care of our dad, it turns out that you've already gone ahead and done it before you realize you couldn't possibly do it, not in a million years.

NOVEMBER 16

He inches around the living room like a spy. He inched off the bed again and got wedged sideways between the bed and the wall. My friend Deirdre spent the night a few days ago and took care of us, and she watched him flailing around in his bassinet and said, "It's so pathetic being a baby, wanting to walk and crawl and run," and I said, "It's like *Johnny Got His Gun,*" and we watched him together for a while. I sort of felt for a minute like I imagine women must feel when they and their husbands watch their baby together. It felt really great, and then I got really sad. Now as I watch he's inching all over the place, obviously trying to implement his plans for world peace.

His eyes are turning brown. Pammy and I went for a walk

along the salt marsh a few days ago. Everything was red with pickleweed, and even though his eyes mostly look blue, in the bright sunlight his pupils were so tiny that you could see that the ring of iris nearest the pupil was definitely turning brown. What a clever baby.

NOVEMBER 22

I wish he could take longer naps in the afternoon. He falls asleep and I feel I could die of love when I watch him, and I think to myself that he is what angels look like. Then I doze off, too, and it's like heaven, but sometimes only twenty minutes later he wakes up and begins to make his gritchy rodent noises, scanning the room wildly. I look blearily over at him in the bassinet, and think, with great hostility, Oh, God, he's raising his loathsome reptilian head again.

When I go over to the bassinet to pick him up, though, he looks up at me like I'm Coco the clown—he beams, and makes raspberries, and does frantic bicycle kicks like he's doing his baby aerobics. Then I feel I can go on.

. . .

I've never been so up and down in my life, so erratic and wild. My body is slowly getting back to normal, except for my butt and thighs. I have to keep remembering the line about the little earth suits and that I am a feminist, because the thighs are just not doing all that well. I lay in the bathtub yesterday looking at them, thinking of entering that annual Hemingway write-alike contest with a piece called, "Thighs Like White Elephants."

And then a part of me thinks, Hey, who fucking cares?

NOVEMBER 23

It's been twenty-six years since John Kennedy was killed. I was in the fifth grade. I had a chopped-olive sandwich for lunch and two Hostess cupcakes. I can remember all that exactly, and yet a few days ago I got into the shower in my underpants. I feel so nostalgic for Kennedy today. We all know now that he had the moral life of a red-ass baboon, but, God almighty, compared to Bush, he's like Desmond Tutu. I wish Sam didn't have to grow up in such a violent scary world. There's so much cancer, so much plague; there are so goddamn many child-snatchers, psychopaths, Republicans. It's all so nuts these days. When did that happen?

Obviously there's a downward spiral going on, that much is clear, and all kinds of good, lovely people keep getting caught in it, while all these shitheads thrive. For instance, Sam and I saw this woman today at the market who is wealthy and obviously doing fabulously well, and everyone toadies up to her and pretends she's just the most marvelous creation, but the truth is that she's got this worm inside of her. She has to keep feeding it grim bits, like mean gossip and bad news about other people. I actually don't even know her name, but I've been pretending to know who she is for so long that I can't possibly ask her. She knows who I am, though, because she has read my books and the articles about me in the local papers. Right after Sam was born, she became only the second person in history to ask who the baby's father was. We talked to her for a few minutes at the butcher counter today, and it was obvious that she had just had her face done again. The startled look was gone, so she looked like a million dollars, but she can make you feel so bad and low with just a look or a few well-chosen words that you end up wanting to cup your hands protectively over your genitals and skulk back home.

The madness is that I always do this little dance for her, wanting to make a good impression. This is the effect that beautiful rich people have on me. I become subservient, all but bowing and scraping and wanting to give them neck rubs. It's crazy. She's just a mean snot. I believe that she'll outlive us all, her family and portfolios will thrive, her pets will never be hit by cars. She's in her late fifties, and her parents are still alive back East. She introduced me to them last year when they came out for a visit, and they look like aging movie stars. The father is as pleased and smarmy as can be, which is maybe the most galling thing of all, because my father, who was so kind, died so young in the world's most terrible way. I don't get it. What am I going to say to Sam when he first notices that things are so fucking unfair? I don't know. Who was it who said that if something is fair, it's probably just a coincidence? I don't know. I think that way deep down I'm a little bit too much like this woman for comfort. My worm is not quite as big as hers, but maybe it will be with age. All I know is that I couldn't wait to get home so I could call Pammy and we could gossip about the face-lift.

NOVEMBER 26

The kitty runs up and down Sam's body all the time now, like she's giving him a lomilomi massage. My older brother and I used to do them on our dad's back when we were young. He'd seen them done in Tokyo when he was a child. I'm not sure *how* he could have seen people get a massage, since his missionary parents were morally opposed to almost everything having to do with bodily pleasure, but when my brother and I were small, my father would stretch out on the living room carpet, and we'd take turns walking on his back. This morning the kitty walked up and down Sam's back slowly for quite some time, seductively, reverently, peering around at his face from time to time as though she were hearing "What Child Is This?" playing on the soundtrack of her tiny kitty mind.

NOVEMBER 28

Sam slept through the night. I don't want to jinx things by saying it too loudly, but it is true. He slept through the night, from 11:30 until 7:00 this morning. It was very confusing at first. My initial thought was that he had died. Then I actually let out a whoop and have been moving joyfully around the house like Julie Andrews on the mountainside in *The Sound of Music* ever since.

People say he's the loveliest baby they've ever seen, even though his hair is falling out. Of course, they also say this to babies who look like water ouzels. Sam really is handsome, with those huge moonbeam eyes and porno lips, but after bad nights I look at him with fear, as if when all his hair falls out, we might see sixes tattooed all over his head.

NOVEMBER 29

He is three months old today and has slept through the night for three nights in a row. He is definitely a keeper. He's so big and talented compared to how he used to be, and I'd sort of like him to stay this size. On our daily walks, Pammy and I see all these toddlers tearing around. They look sort of unattractively huge and lunky, like loud screamy poopy variations on Diane Arbus's "Jewish Giant." Sam is so delicate.

We are almost completely broke. I don't feel like writing, and I do not have anything to say. I'm trying to stay faithful, even though it makes me feel a little bit like a loser to be broke and fearful. I found myself having the nightmare vision again, where we end up living in the Tenderloin and I have to be a prostitute and walk the streets holding my stomach in, and the baby gets gnawed on by rats and we don't even have a phone. What an incredible drug fear is. My friend Bettie, who goes to my church and is very black and very radical and about ten years older than me, suggested I try to keep my eyes on Jesus. Sometimes I remember to. Other times I'm not sure I really believe in God. It would be best not to overthink it. Otherwise I could become like that dyslexic agnostic in the old joke—the one who lies in bed and tries to figure out if his dog exists.

Movies played in my head today where I could see myself having a drink to wash away the fear of impending financial doom. I saw myself sipping a small and lovely glass of good Scotch. The problem is that I have never sipped a drink in my life. I'm more of a swiller. I did not sip beer at twelve years old, I did not sip drinks at twenty. I didn't even sip the barium milkshake I had to take when I was thirty and getting an ulcer; I swilled it.

NOVEMBER 30

Sam's father filed court papers today saying that we never fucked and that he therefore cannot be the father.

I am trying to get him to sign a paternity stipulation, which just says that I am the mother and that he is the father and that I have custody. I want it partly because Sam is entitled to know who he is and partly because if the guy dies before Sam is eighteen, Sam will be eligible for Social Security.

The thing is that I slept with Sam's father three times a week for three months and with no one else. It's so weird and dreamlike that he's Sam father, but it is the truth. Certainly, though, in the police lineup of my ex-boyfriends, he's probably one of the better donors, tall and brilliant, and Sam's got his gorgeous hair.

As I was writing this, Sam, who is lying beside me on the futon in the living room, suddenly did this fantastic and joyful scream, exactly like James Brown. I don't have any idea what I will tell Sam when he is old enough to ask about his father. I'll say that everybody doesn't have *some*thing and that he doesn't have this one thing, but that we have each other and that is a lot. And that for a while his father was my friend.

Peg came over and took three huge loads of laundry to the Laundromat. She brought us this amazing breakfast that was left over from one of her catering gigs, a sandwich made of cream cheese and lots of blueberries, which you turned into French toast by dipping it into egg and frying it so that the cream cheese melted all over the warm blueberries, and then you put syrup on top. It was so good it brought tears to my eyes. I had to eat Sam's portion, too, because he has no teeth.

I asked her if she had any thoughts on how to help Sam deal

with not having a dad, and she repeated what her AA friends say, that more will be revealed, meaning that when the time comes, I will know what to do. She also pointed out that Sam wouldn't be talking in real sentences for a couple of years and that maybe there were more immediate things that I could mind-fuck to death.

It's so hard to keep my sticky little fingers off the controls of this spaceship, especially when I get scared, like now when God has not bothered to give me the specific details of his solution to our financial needs. I'm just a little edgy being in the dark about it. I don't understand why he always has to be so goddamn weird about his plans. I would prefer that he be more like Jeeves, streaming into rooms like sunlight with all that I need to feel comfortable—God as cosmic butler. This other way is so hard. It always reminds me of the man who has fallen off a cliff but managed to grab onto a weak vine. Holding it, watching it begin to come loose, he looks up toward the top of the cliff and cries out for help. Suddenly, a deep booming voice from the sky says gently to him, "It is all right, my son. I am here and will never let harm befall you. Just let go of the vine, and fall into my arms. I will catch you." The surprised man thinks about this for a moment, looks down at the ground thousands of feet below, then up to the ledge above him, clears his throat, and asks, "Is there anybody else up there?"

I have a deep belief that I know what is best for me and

now, by extension, what is best for Sam. The fact that I have spent my life proving that just the opposite is true does not keep me from acting like a schizophrenic traffic cop with a mission and a bullhorn. There's something sort of poignantly ludicrous about it. I heard this old man speak when I was pregnant, someone who had been sober for fifty years, a very prominent doctor. He said that he'd finally figured out a few years ago that his profound sense of control, in the world and over his life, is another addiction and a total illusion. He said that when he sees little kids sitting in the backseat of cars, in those car seats that have steering wheels, with grim expressions of concentration on their faces, clearly convinced that their efforts are causing the car to do whatever it is doing, he thinks of himself and his relationship with God: God who drives along silently, gently amused, in the real driver's seat.

December 1

Sam turned over from his stomach to his back yesterday, and then he forgot how. Later I saw him tugging at his chin like he was trying to remember. At any rate, he hasn't done it again.

He is a very good but very needy baby. He coos and roars

his baby roar and tugs Hasidically at his chin. I know it's too early for him to be teething, but he is as drooly as a Newfoundland. Everything goes into his mouth. Everything gets gummed to death. We give him bagels to gum, and he works them over with a kind of frantic joy—I think he's doing his impersonation of Dan Quayle eating.

DECEMBER 2

It has been a terrible day. I'm afraid I'm going to have to let him go. He's an awful baby. I hate him. He's scum.

Midnight

I'm not even remotely well enough to be a mother. That's what the problem is. Also, I don't think I like babies.

Pammy came by late in the afternoon and saved the day. Emmy dropped by with groceries. I felt like I could hardly be nice to Sam because I was so tired and he was such a kvetchy little bundle of shitty diapers and bad attitude. And then while Pammy was supposed to be keeping an eye on him, he inched his way off the futon and did a double gainer onto the floor. He just entirely lost his mind. So I was called in to comfort him, and of course I fell right back in love. I said to Pammy, "Well, there goes your standing in the community. You used to be number two for him, I think," and she said, "Yeah, and now I'm number twenty-nine, right between George Bush and the nurse who gave him his DPTs."

We sat outside, and it was so breathtakingly green under the redwoods. All the birds were singing, and Sam fell asleep in my arms. Pammy made us lemonade. It was like a glimpse of paradise. I was not exaggerating when I said earlier that when I was drinking and using I couldn't take decent care of a cat, so all this feels like a small miracle—and not even such a small one, maybe a medium-sized one in plain brown paper.

I saw a "60 Minutes" show a few years ago about Lourdes, with Ed Bradley interviewing a family of three who came to the shrine every year—a devoutly religious mother of about thirty, a much much older father who could barely look at the camera and who couldn't say one word because he was so terribly shy, and a little ten-year-old girl with spina bifada who was in a wheelchair. They came to Lourdes every single year, and Ed Bradley was kind of badgering the parents for being so gullible. He said to the little girl, who was so weak she had to be firmly strapped into the wheelchair, "What do you pray for when you come?" and she said, looking at her father really lovingly, "I pray that my dad won't always have to feel so shy. It makes him feel so lonely." Which stopped old Ed in his tracks for about ten seconds. But then he looked back at the mother and said something to the effect that "year after year, you spend thousands and thousands of dollars to come here, hoping for a miracle," and she just looked at her kid, shook her head, and said, "Oh, no, Ed, you don't get it—we *got* our miracle."

DECEMBER 3

Sam was baptized today at Saint Andrew's. It is almost too painful to talk about, so powerful, so outrageous and lovely. Just about every person I adore was there. They were the exact people I would invite to my wedding.

Everyone cried, or at any rate, lots of people did—all those old faces of the people at my church, and all the younger people, too, and my family and best friends, everyone clapping and singing along with the choir. All these old left-wing atheist friends singing gospel music. The singing was extraordinary, the choir of these beautiful black women and one white man, singing to Sam and me. A friend of nearly twenty years,

Neshama, from Bolinas, described the two of us as looking very tremulous and white and cherished. Out of this broken-down old church, out of the linoleum floors and the crummy plastic stained-glass windows, came the most wonderful sounds anyone had ever heard, because of the spirit that moved the day.

Sam was just great, although I must say I took the liberty of dosing him with perhaps the merest hint of Tylenol beforehand so he wouldn't weep or whine too much during the service. He wore the baptism gown that my cousin Samuel had worn fifty years ago, very Bonnie Prince Charlie, very lacy and high Episcopalian, with a plain little white cap.

For the huge party at Pammy's afterward, he changed into his one-piece cow outfit. It was a wonderful party. Everybody mingled like mad, except me, and everyone got to hang out in the garden because it was such a beautiful day. I kept feeling that God was really showing off. The party felt like the secular portion of the show.

I've always kept the various parts of my life compartmentalized, but today all the important people from all aspects of my life were finally brought together: my sweet nutty family, in droves; my reading group; people I have worked with at magazines over the years; old lovers; and the women I have loved most in my life. It was my tribe. It felt like Brownian motion, all of these friends who had been strangers to one another bumping off each other in the garden.

Inside Pammy's house, the sun streamed through the windows, and there were vases of flowers everywhere, dozens of vases, hundreds of flowers of every possible color and shade, some arranged as if by pros, some like crazy hairdos. It was like a Haight-Ashbury wedding. Emmy and Bill brought a whole roast turkey, and everyone else brought the most beautiful dish he or she knew how to make. Mom and Dudu had been in charge of recruiting the food, and there were beautiful bowls and plates of food on every inch of tabletop and counter. My brilliant old friend Leroy from Petaluma, who has been a permanent member of my food review squad for years, told my mother that the food was so exquisite that after eating, one heard the "Triumphal March" from Verdi's *Aida*, had visions of elephants, camels, cannons. My mother was so proud, so high from the whole thing that she could have chased down an airplane.

The kid made a haul, fantastic toys and clothes and books for the little emir. Dudu and Rex started a savings account for him; my reading group gave us a check for a small fortune. Except for the fact that there was folk music on the stereo, it was like the wedding scene in *The Godfather*.

A bunch of other babies were there, all of them about Sam's age, and they were all so much more robust than Sam. He is a skinny little guy. When I mentioned this to Neshama, she said very kindly that the other babies looked like babies on steroids while Sam was a baby on spirit. I had to hide in a back room with him practically the whole time because I was too overwhelmed, amazed, and profoundly grateful at how loved Sam is and how loved I am. It made my stomach ache.

Now I am sitting here on the futon in the living room, Sam asleep beside me, the kitty sniffing at him with enormous interest as if I had accidentally brought a perfectly broiled Rock Cornish game hen to bed with me. I have spent so much of my life with secret Swiss-cheese insides, but I tell you—right now, Mama, my soul is full.

DECEMBER 5

Pammy showed me a picture that someone took at the baptism of her holding Sam out toward the camera. He definitely looks like he was blown away by the proceedings, too, somehow sort of blank and surprised at the same time, like he had just that moment been plucked from a huge pie.

All these people keep waxing sentimental about how fabulously well I am doing as a mother, how competent I am, but

I feel inside like when you're first learning to put nail polish on your right hand with your left. You can *do* it, but it doesn't look all that great around the cuticles. And I think that because I'm so tired all the time, people feel like I'm sort of saintly. But the shadow knows. The other night I was nursing the baby outside, underneath the redwoods, and you could see the full moon in the clearing of the treetops. Everything smelled so clean and green, and the night birds were singing, and then I started feeling a little edgy about money or the lack thereof. I started feeling sorry for myself because I'm tired and broke, kept thinking that what this family needs is a breadwinner. And pretty soon my self-esteem wasn't very good, and I felt that maybe secretly I'm sort of a loser. So when my friend John called a few minutes later from L.A. and mentioned that a mutual friend of ours, whose first book was out (for which he had been grossly overpaid, if you ask me), had gotten a not-very-good review in *Newsweek* recently, all of a sudden, talking on the cordless phone and nursing my baby in the moonlight, I had a wicked, dazzling bout of schadenfreude. Schadenfreude is that wicked and shameful tickle of pleasure one feels at someone else's misfortune. It felt like I'd gotten a little hit of something. It made me feel better about myself. "Do you have it?" I asked innocently, and he said that he didn't think so because it was a week or so old. I then found myself clearing my throat and saying in a flat, innocently curious voice, "Why don't you go look?" So he did, and returned to the phone with it, and I said, nice as pie, "Now read it." And when he was done, I said, "Man, that was like *Christ*mas for me." Then we laughed, and it was okay for a minute.

God, it was painful though, too, and the hangover was debilitating. I was deeply aware of the worm inside of *me* and of the grim bits that I feed it. The secret envy inside me is maybe the worst thing about my life. I am the Saddam Hussein of jealousy. But the grace is that there are a couple of people I can tell it to without them staring at me as if I have fruit bats flying out of my nose, who just nod, and maybe laugh, and say, Yep, yep, I get it, I'm the same. Still, I feel like it must drive Jesus just out of his mind sometimes, that instead of loving everyone like he or she is my sibling, with a heart full of goodwill and tenderness and forgiveness, I'm secretly scheming and thinking my dark greedy thoughts. I say to him, Bear with me, dude. He does give me every single thing I need, but then I still want more, and I picture him stamping around like Danny DeVito, holding up these gnarled beseeching hands of frustration, saying, "Oy fucking *veh.*"

DECEMBER 6

We had a great time today. He slept a lot, laughed a lot, played, roared. Later we had a Hoagy Carmichael dance contest, and we won—we won big. It was just Sam, the kitty, and me, but still, we felt good about it.

It takes Sam a long time to fall asleep at night, and when he does, I can't tiptoe around cleaning up because (I think) he subconsciously hears me sneaking around and finds it unbecoming and he wakes up crying. So often I just sit by him and watch him sleep. I tell him while he sleeps that it's a jungle out there, and you have to be really, really careful or else the eagles will get you, like they got Johnny G. My friend Mary had six cats at one point, until her cat Johnny G. disappeared, and eagles had been seen in the sky that very same day, so of course you could only draw one conclusion. After that she used always to warn the other cats to be really careful so that the eagles didn't get them, too. The odds seemed so stacked. Have you ever seen that awful PBS nature movie on baby turtles, where they show you the beach where twenty million turtle eggs are laid and then hatch? Then they show you those twenty million baby turtles trying to race across the sand before the seagulls swoop down and gobble them up. About forty-five baby turtles make it to the water. It makes you shake your head. You double over and have to hold onto your stomach. I say, Please, please, please, God, let Sam make it to the water.

He can roll over to one side and no longer just says, Ah-goo. He does all these fabulous babbles and bellowings now. He's so pretty that it's sort of nuts. I'm sure he will be as gay as an Easter bonnet. My friend Larry gave him a naked Ken doll that Sam took a shine to one evening when my reading group met at Larry's, and it's totally Fire Island around here now. Sam licks and chews the naked Ken doll at every opportunity. I called Larry and said, "You're trying to recruit my son," and he said, "Look at it this way—in twenty years you won't be losing a son; you'll be gaining a son." Larry has AIDS, or at any rate has HIV and no T-cell count these days. Boy, talk about the baby turtles. I worry that he won't be here when Sam is four or five. Of course, I don't know if I'll be here, either. Larry called one night at the end of my pregnancy when I was just devastated by the thought of the hole in Sam's life because he wouldn't have a dad, how much that was probably going to hurt and how I wasn't going to be able to do much about it. He said that I was just an opening for Sam to come into the world, that I wasn't supposed to be a drug for him. I was just supposed to be his mother. Sam was meant to be born into the world exactly the way it is, into these exact circumstances, even if that meant not having a dad or an ozone layer, even if it included pets who would die and acne and seventh-grade dances and AIDS. He simply wasn't meant to be born in the paradise behind the mountains.

DECEMBER 7

I woke him last night at 12:30 to nurse him, and he looked at me like "Are you out of your fucking *mind?*" But then he nursed for a long time. He woke up at 4:00, but I gave him his pacifier, patted him, and told him what a good kitty-cat he was, and he fell right back to sleep until 9:00. So I feel like a million dollars, like I am on the road to a complete recovery. Steve came by with take-out Mexican food tonight and after dinner sat talking to Sam about life while I took a bath. I eavesdropped: Steve said that meeting Sam was one of the best things that had ever happened to him but that another was having finally learned to swim at the age of thirty. "Life is really great sometimes," he said. The fact that he couldn't swim was always this deep secret that Steve went to great lengths to hide, like the men and women who can't read or write but who have all these fabulous tricks and games they play to keep their illiteracy a secret.

Then this summer Steve did one of the bravest things I've ever heard of. He took swimming lessons where all these kids could watch him. He said it was like learning to ride a bike when you're thirty years old and six-foot-three, with a bunch of kids on skateboards looking on.

But he did it. He learned to swim. He was telling Sam tonight that he went around for all these years dreading that somehow he would be found out, someone would have a foolproof way to get him into the ocean or into a pool, and he'd have to admit he couldn't swim. And now he can.

Now there's only this one other little secret that he has. He can't start barbecues, which of course everyone in California is expected to be able to do. Stacking the briquettes, sprinkling in the charcoal lighter, letting the coals get red hot and then white—you know, the whole Gestalt. So now he's afraid that he'll be at some pool party, finally splashing around happily in the pool, maybe doing a few nonchalant laps, and someone will holler, "Hey, Steve! Why don't you come do me a favor and get the charcoals started?"

DECEMBER 9

Sam's getting a lot of hand control. He can grasp the rattle if you touch the backs of his fingers with it. Before, you had to spread his fingers open and wedge the rattle in. It always made me think of those movies where the dead person is clutching a coin or a clue in their rigor-mortised hand and the detective has to pry the fingers open. But this morning I took this weird black elastic-Lego-bell contraption that looks like a molecular model and put it on Sam's stomach. The next thing I knew he was banging himself euphorically in the face.

It's also National Sam Lamott Neck Control Day. We're talking major, hard-core neck control. I changed our answering machine to say, "We're apparently out celebrating National Sam Lamott Improved Neck Control Week, but operators are standing by to take your call . . ." People left the most supportive messages, as if Sam had triumphed over muscular dystrophy, like "All *right*, babe—*go* for it." Larry's message said, "Oh, it's all too much for me. Please give the little savant a *huge* hug from all of us."

December 17

I did a terrible thing yesterday. Someone had invited us to a birthday party that I totally did not want to go to. I just hate parties so much. I'm always reminded of that wonderful Virginia Woolf line where she says she and her sister Vanessa would go to parties and end up sitting there like deaf-mutes waiting for the funeral to begin. I really couldn't think of a way out of this party because it was for someone I really love. But then Sam started crying hysterically because he was so tired and strung out, and a light bulb went on over my head, and I rushed to the phone with him in my arms, wailing, and called the friend. I said Sam and I were both exhausted and just couldn't possibly come, and the woman said, "Oh, well, of course we're terribly disappointed," but I could tell she was desperately relieved. She probably got off the phone going, "Oh, thank you Jesus, *thank* you, *thank* you."

CHRISTMAS EVE

We all had Christmas Eve with Dudu and Rex, as we have for about thirty years now, although this, of course, was Sam's first year. They are so desperately in love with him. I worry that they have come to think of me as his driver. I felt such a deep sadness that my father didn't get to know Sam. The last Christmas my dad was alive, he was fifty-four and had been sick for a year and half, he looked very handsome in his best L. L. Bean clothes, but his brain didn't work so well anymore. The awareness of how much ground he had lost made him unbearably sad and worried. It was the hardest thing for me, definitely harder even than knowing that he would be dead pretty soon. Luckily, we three Lamott kids were all still drinking heavily at the time, so we ended up having a tipsy, if not happy, night. I wish now I could have been more present for my dad's sickness. I was drunk and high every night. That last Christmas I kept praying for God to pull a rabbit out of his hat and come up with some sort of solution, and about two weeks later Dad was definitely much more senile, beyond even noticing that his brain was shot, so it wasn't a great solution, if you ask me. Still, it was better than nothing. I guess that's about all you get sometimes. I remember at one point on that last Christmas Eve he had a bright quilted tea cozy on his head, like a crown, and he really looked great, like he was having a good time.

Anyway, tonight Sam wore a red tuxedo sleeper with a black bow tie that Julie and John from upstairs gave us. Steve said he looked like a toreador. He always sleeps through the night now, and when he's awake he lies around and makes raspberries and plays with his feet. He has even stuck them in his mouth twice now. Obviously he is an extremely gifted baby. He's terribly drooly and may be teething. And also—this is almost too much to handle—when I hold him now, he puts an arm around my neck. It's very casual. He just kind of slings his arm around me, like he's Sam Shepard or something. It makes me woozy.

CHRISTMAS

We had a perfect Christmas. Steve, Sam, and I went out to Stinson Beach for the whole day with Bill Turnbull, my publisher at North Point, and his wife, who is my other mother. We went for a long walk on the beach and then watched *The Godfather II* and ate hot-fudge sundaes.

I swear I have never felt so aware of God as I did walking on the beach with these people, who are atheists, with Sam on my back making raspberries. I know we all only talk about God in the most flat-footed way, but I suddenly had that Old Testament sense of God's presence, a kind of weighty presence in the midst of all this tumultuous weather and surf. Even when the feeling was gone, I was left with the sense that something is here with us, something that is big and real and protective.

I do sometimes feel intensely aware of a presence and a voice so pure that they just couldn't have come from this world.

DECEMBER 27

He does this worried-hand thing now with his fingers and hands, the fingertips and nails of one hand clicking rapidly against those of the other, so he looks just like he's knitting.

Also, when he's on his stomach, he'll suddenly sort of sag forward in a rolling motion because he wants to move but he can't quite keep his head up. It's some kind of precrawling

thing, and it makes him look exactly like a sow bug. I mean
that in the nicest possible way.

Dudu and Rex's daughter Carmen and I sat around all morning eating Christmas chocolates and playing with the baby and
laughing about our mothers. I was just in heaven. I've known
Dudu since I was born, and Carmie has known my mother
since she was three, so we feel it's okay for us to laugh about
them. We do impersonations of their sometimes fierce, sometimes passive-aggressive attempts to influence how we ought to
live. I keep remembering a letter Simone Weil wrote to her
mother in France, when the mother was panic-stricken because
Simone was doing all this radical social-activist work with the
poor, even though she (Simone) was very frail, very sick.
Simone said to her mother something like "I love you, and if
I had two lives, I would give you one. But I don't." The awful thing is that Sam will probably get hold of this line someday, too.

DECEMBER 31

Today is Pammy's thirty-fifth birthday. Sam and I don't have any big New Year's Eve plans. We'll probably have another dance contest, and we'll probably win it again. We're that good. What I hope for the new year is that Sam has a great ride and that I learn to stay a little bit more in the now. I noticed the other day that not only do I spend a lot of the time in the future with imaginary triumphs and catastrophes and boyfriends, or in the past with my memories, but I'm so crazy that sometimes I even go into the past and rehash things that turned out *well* yet *might* have turned out disastrously. For instance, the car that almost hit us last month might not have managed to stop in time, and I'd be in a hospital with casts on all four limbs, IVs, cannulas up my nose, looking very thin and pale but sort of ethereally lovely, and I'd have to learn to walk all over again using computers and enormous force of character, and I'd be a really good sport about it all and get to be on "60 Minutes." I used to have a lot of these fantasies, of being badly hurt but being loved back to health and being incredibly brave and spiritual about the whole thing, like Beth in *Little Women.* I think these fantasies were about trying to get people to see how hurt I was on the inside, even though my outsides looked okay. I don't know. I do it only about half as much since Sam was born.

Maybe there just isn't time. There's also not much time anymore to look in the mirror, which I used to do quite a lot in a casual sort of way: I'd check myself out every time I used the bathroom, to make contact with myself a little, like "Hey, nice to see you, how you doing, babe, looking good," or else I'd fixate on how old I am getting, how I'm beginning to look like Georgia O'Keeffe with an Afro. It's that radio station KFKD, K-Fucked, which plays in stereo in my head: out of the right speaker, the endless self-aggrandizement, all the commentary regarding my specialness, uniqueness, all the imaginary TV talk-show interviews with Johnny and Joan and Dick Cavett, and then out of the left speaker, all the mind-fucking, every late-breaking bad bulletin on what a mess I'm making or am about to make of things, the fear of being uncovered, of impending doom. So I try to change channels, out of my head where the station plays and into my heart, and my wish for this year is that I remember to change channels more often.

Sam's Big Brother Brian, who still takes him every Tuesday for a few hours, is married to a very funny Southern woman named Diane, who's bleached fabulously blonde, sober fifteen years, very Eve Ardenish. She says that we're all so nuts amid so much beauty that it's like we're at the circus. In one ring is an amazing array of clowns and bears doing all this great stuff, and in the middle ring is a woman who does breathtaking tricks on horseback, and in the far ring are elephants or seals and maybe more clowns, and above us are trapeze artists, doing these death-defying precision feats, and we're sitting in our seats looking around crabbily, going, "Where's that damn peanut vendor? I want my goddamn peanuts!"—even when we're not particularly hungry.

But, oh, God, all I really care about is that the eagles don't get Sam like they got Johnny G. He's lying on his stomach beside me on a bright-blue comforter, doing the sow-bug rolling-forward motion, flailing his arms, roaring and hollering. He appears to be bodysurfing in the tropics. You can almost hear the Beach Boys singing "Help Me, Rhonda" in the background.

JANUARY 4

There are huge changes every day now. Maybe there always were, but I was too tired to notice. His main activities currently are nursing, foot sucking, making raspberries and bubbles, and chewing on his Odie doll's ear. We were sitting out beneath the moon again, nursing, and it occurred to me that someday he will stare at the full moon and know the word for it.

Things are getting better now. They've been easier for a month. People kept telling me that I just had to hold on until the end of the third month and everything would get easier. I always thought they were patronizing me or trying to keep me from scrounging up cab fare to the bridge. But I remember a month ago, when he turned three months and one or two days—it was like the baby looked at his little watch calendar and said with a bit of surprise, "Oh, for Chrissakes, it's been three months already—time to chill out a little." He sleeps every night, and doesn't cry or gritch very often, and just in general seems to be enjoying his stay a little bit more. It's much better. I'm much better. This guy I know who is really nuts and really spiritual said the other day, "My mind is a bad neighborhood that I try not to go into alone." That pretty much says it for me in the first three months.

My friend Michelle calls the first three months the fourth trimester.

Another thing I notice is that I'm much less worried all the time—a lot of things are no big deal now, whereas in the beginning everything was. For instance, now Sam can go for a few days without pooping, or can poop ten times in one day, without my automatically thinking he has some terrible intestinal blockage or deformity that will require a colostomy, and that will make trying to get him into day care a living hell.

He's becoming so grown-up before my very eyes. It's so painful. I want him to stay this age forever.

I look at him all the time and think, "Where'd you come from?" as if out of the blue, some Bouvier puppy came to live here with me and the kitty. I don't really know how it happened. It seems like I was just sitting around reading a book, and what book it was I can't remember, and then all of a sudden, here he is, sucking on his foot and his Odie doll's ear.

He has this beautiful hand gesture where, when he's nursing, he reaches back with his free hand to touch and lightly pat the crown of his head, and it looks exactly like he's checking to see if his bald spot is exposed.

JANUARY 9

I'm mental and defeated and fat and loathsome and I am crazily, brain-wastedly tired. I couldn't sleep. This is maybe the loneliest I have ever felt. It's lonelier than Dad's last few months, when his brain was all gone. At least he used to sleep through the night.

Later in the Day

We're a little better. Emmy came by with groceries and took care of Sam while I took a bath. Then we both slept for a while this afternoon, and when I woke up, I lay nursing him with lots of covers on us, thinking about the Special Olympics. I'm not sure why. I've gone to them for five or six years in a row now. They're held in the spring at the College of Marin, and as I lay nursing Sam, I saw movies in my head of all the times over the years during the track-and-field events when runners have stopped halfway down the track, out of confusion or exhaustion or pain or whatever, and just sat down in the dirt. Sometimes they sit there completely frozen, staring at the sky, and sometimes they start to take their shoes or clothes off just because, I think, they don't know what else to do. Every single one of them has been assigned a volunteer, though, and that person steps out from the sidelines and goes to the runner, and gets down on the ground with him or her and helps him or her put the shoes and clothes back on, and then takes the person by the hand and they start off again toward the finish line. In all the years I've been going, I've never once seen someone not get over the finish line. Right now, I feel very aware of all the volunteers God's given to me, because I tell you, I've ended up on my butt in the dirt a *lot* these last few months. I ended up there again this morning. Now I'm back on my feet, more or less.

JANUARY 10

I bet that life must be like a dream for Sam. It must be such a surprise for him to wake up every morning and for the whole thing to still be going on, the same way it must have been a joy and a surprise every morning for the primitives when the sun came up again.

JANUARY 12

A big day here at home. Sam rolled over five or six times from his stomach to his back, followed each time by lovely squeals and the James Brown shrieks. Also, he can now hold his little plastic book up so that it looks like he's reading thoughtfully. Sometimes he looks up toward the ceiling, with a pondering frown, exactly like William F. Buckley.

He is lying beside me now, reading his plastic Beatrix Potter bath book, very absorbed. I try to get his attention, but I can see that I am just annoying the shit out of him.

. . .

Tonight we went to Bolinas to visit Sylvie, my ninety-year-old Swiss novelist friend who had knit, with her ancient gnarled hands, a beautiful little yellow coat for Sam, with a collar and little knit buttons. So I went out to take her some dinner and to show off the baby in his yellow knit coat. It's a little like something Liberace might have worn at three months old, but Sam is such a manly guy that he can pull it off. So we were driving over the mountain, and on our side it was blue and sunny, but as soon as we crested, I could see the thickest blanket of fog I've ever seen, so thick it was quilted with the setting sun shining upward from underneath it, and it shimmered with reds and roses, and above were radiant golden peach colors. I am not exaggerating this. I haven't seen a sky so stunning and bejeweled and shimmering with sunset colors and white lights since the last time I took LSD, ten years ago. But do you want to know my very first thought upon seeing this? I thought, Oh, shit, the fog's coming in—the ride home will be a pain in the neck. And then, right that second, I got it. I started laughing at myself, and pulled the car over and got out, and got the baby out of his car seat, and we stood looking for a while till it got too cold.

Sylvie was absolutely blown away by how beautiful and good Sam is.

Now he's on his stomach in his bassinet. It's 10:00 at night and he's sort of lurching around but not crying, and he keeps raising his head to look around, like a turtle.

JANUARY 15

Last night we were driving to the grocery store, and he was falling asleep in his car seat. When we got to the parking lot of the store, I said his name loudly to wake him up. He was halfway between sleep and wakefulness, and suddenly his eyes rolled all the way back in his head, and he shuddered, and I decided in a split second that he was having a massive seizure. I couldn't breathe, and when, two seconds later, he wouldn't rouse, I slapped his face! And he startled awake and looked at me like my nasal hairs were on fire. He burst into tears. I took him out of his seat and comforted him, and then we went into the store.

Back at home, he fell right to sleep. I was starving to death and felt like my body was cannibalizing itself, and I desperately wanted to cook while he slept. But I kept dropping things—a mug, a huge slotted metal spoon—right next to his bassinet. Each time he'd startle and almost wake up, while I'd stand there holding my breath, and then I'd try to be more careful. I felt like I was underwater. I was trying to do everything while wearing oven mitts on both hands. Then I actually dropped a *pan* on the floor, and it reverberated like a huge gong you might use to summon the Dalai Lama to dinner, and I just turned on myself viciously and said, "Why don't you just fucking *slap* him again?" I ended up so mad at myself, so

impatient, and that sent me into this terrible feeling of aloneness. Sam kept sleeping.

Later I found this Polaroid I'd taken when I was about seven
months pregnant and feeling psychotically alone and incom-
plete because my other four friends who were having babies were
spending all this time getting the *nurseries* together, with their
husbands, their doting, excited husbands. And I felt like the lonely
hunchback innkeeper who had somehow gotten knocked up.
But then two very old black women at my church—Alma, the
one who wears the little ersatz Coco Chanel outfits, and Mary
Williams, who calls me "sugar" and blesses me ("Bless you,
sugar, bless you, bless you")—had both stuffed a bunch of bills
into the pocket of my coat. They each live on about $600 a
month. It humbled me. It sort of kicked the shit out of my
feeling sorry for myself. When I got home, I'd found the
sonogram picture of Sam when he was a four-month-old fetus,
and a picture of me at thirty-five holding the kitty, and a picture
of me at seven years old, because I can still feel that girl inside my
soul, and I taped them all under the arms of the crucifix in my
kitchen. Then I took a Polaroid close-up of the whole scene and
carried it in my wallet for the rest of my pregnancy, as my family
portrait—me, Jesus, Sam, and the little seven-year-old girl. I'd
say to myself, See? We are already a complete family unit. We
don't need some guy. We are whole.

I'd forgotten I had it. I had hidden it away so they couldn't
use it against me at my commitment hearings.

We are almost out of money. I have eight hundred dollars left in my savings account. The only money I am making is the thousand a month for the *California* food review. I have Megan for a few hours every day and cannot possibly give that up. It's seven bucks an hour, but it is cheap at twice the price. It has given me a whole new lease on life. I can't figure out any places where we can cut back. The friends who do the food reviews with me every month are already paying for their own dinners so that I can pocket the expense check. If worse comes to worst, Pammy and her husband could lend me some money until I am back in the saddle financially. I wrote a note to God this morning. I said that I did not have any solutions to my money problems, that I can and will scratch around and find some free-lance gigs if that is what his will for me is—that is, as opposed to settling down and trying to get an advance for a new book—but that in the meantime I need my next operating instructions. I folded it up and put it in the little box by my bed. Then I sat by the phone for about five minutes, primly, with my knees together and my hands folded in my lap, waiting, because I couldn't think of anything else to do.

Nothing happened, except that Megan arrived for work and

found me sitting like that. It was a little bit embarrassing. She cocked her head and after a moment said, "Are you expecting a call?" and I said, "Yes," and she said, "From who?" and I said I really didn't know. She nodded quite respectfully and went off to get the baby.

They spent the morning at the park, and I got to work on my food review. It was a great salve for the fear. The Smiths and Peg and Leroy and I had gone out a week ago to this happening place on the Embarcadero that everyone said was supposed to be a lot of fun. ("Oh, great," said Leroy, bitterly, "a lot of *fun?* Shall I bring my little piece of the Berlin wall?") And it *was* fun, partly because the food was so bad. It turned out to be a really funny review. I am grateful for the easy money, but I need $1,500 a month more to get by. Megan came back from the park with the baby at noon and asked, "Did your call come through?" and I shook my head, and she thought about this for a moment and said, "Well? Maybe tomorrow."

She is really interested in a new man. I can hardly remember what that feels like. As I recall, half the time it's fantastic and you feel larger than life and you have this marvelous cell membrane around the two of you and you dream your dreamy dreams of running in slow motion through the fields into the arms of your beloved, and the rest of the time you're totally

143

fucked up the ass, breathing asthmatically if at all, psychically doubled over on the floor with little rivulets of barf trickling down from the corners of your mouth.

Megan, at twenty-two, seems so grounded. She's taking it slow, although she admitted that sometimes there's a certain temptation to do just the opposite, to throw caution to the wind and move in together and create all that delicious drama. I told her something my friend Deirdre said last year about the man I was seeing before I got involved with Sam's father. She was urging me to go slow and not to make any commitment to the guy or to want one until we'd gone out for months and months. She said, Think of it as having come upon a beautiful canoe on the shore. Now, no matter how much you want to get in it and paddle way out into the water, maybe all the way across the Pacific, no matter how long you've had to wait to do so, you simply don't do it. You'd paddle around the shore for a while, maybe for weeks, take little excursions, test it out. Maybe it would seem okay the first few times, but then it might turn out to be full of tiny holes and cracks and start to sink, and you would need to bail. It would have turned out that you had gotten the last good hours out of that beautiful shitty little boat. It was a good thing that you hadn't gone out very far.

J A N U A R Y 2 4

I gave Sam a little rice cereal tonight strictly out of boredom. It used to be that *I* overate when I was bored, but now I get to overfeed the baby. He's lovelier, funnier, smarter, and more alert every day. Everyone says so. He laughs out loud a lot, sucks on his feet, and makes these screams of joy and amazement that sometimes scare the kitty half to death. She'll be walking up to him right when he lets out a banshee scream, and it's exactly like in the cartoons, she leaps straight into the air and looks like she's been electrocuted. Then a little later I'll find her curled up next to him licking his ears.

I think she thinks that he is hers. I remember how I used to have these anxiety attacks about the kitty putting a pillow on top of the baby's face while he slept or pinching his little nostrils and mouth shut. That's why I like that line so much about my mind being a bad neighborhood I shouldn't go into alone. It's too often 4:00 A.M. in one's mind, the hour of the black dogs, and there are so many muggers and drive-by shootings and piles of dog shit you step in just when you're starting to feel better about things. One's heart is the only safe place to be. There's light there, there's company, and quiet.

That same bad-neighborhood guy said, smiling in this nice self-deprecating way, "Hey, I may not be much, but I'm all I think about."

JANUARY 26

There's been a miracle here, the sort of thing that you could not get away with in fiction. Your editor would say, "Look, I'm sorry, but no one would believe it. Things just don't happen like that in real life." What happened is, a woman named Liz Logan, who used to be an editor at 7 *Days* magazine, called me this morning. We have corresponded once or twice because she is a fan of my books and restaurant reviews. She just got hired as the articles editor at *Mademoiselle*, and she offered me the book column this morning, for two thousand dollars a month. Two thousand dollars a month! God Almighty.

I can't contain myself. It makes me want to have a whole bunch of cigarettes or something. Pammy is on her way over with the makings for hot-fudge sundaes. Gonna get *down*.

"Oh, Sam," I said to him when I hung up from talking to Pammy, "honey?" But I couldn't put how I felt into words, so I ran into our funny little bedroom, buried my head in a pillow, and cried.

JANUARY 27

Sam eats rice cereal and carrots every day and makes bright orange poops. Feeding him is like filling a hole with putty—you get it in and then you sort of shave off all the excess around the hole and gob it back in, like you're spackling.

JANUARY 28

Everyone is ecstatic because of *Mademoiselle.* Everyone called everyone else to discuss the big news, and then everyone called me. It has been a great couple of days, with much jubilation. It feels like the worst is over. I wish I could tell my dad. It makes me remember the only lines from the Bible that I know for sure he loved, from Song of Solomon, chapter two, "For, lo, the winter is past, the rain is over and gone; The flowers appear on the earth; the time of the singing of birds is come, and the voice of the turtle is heard in our land." My father would raise a fist, and beam.

JANUARY 29

Another birthday. He's five months old. He can do all sorts of brilliant things now besides squealing and sucking his feet. His new thing is that he scratches absolutely everything with all the fingers of one hand at once—the material of the couch, my chest, the sheet of his bassinet, which, against the plastic-covered foam pad, sounds like "scritch scritch scritch." It's sort of spasmodic and eerie, because in the silence those tiny little fingers are the only things moving. It sounds like someone who has been buried alive and is scratching the top of a coffin. "Stop doing that," I say, "it's wearing on my nerves," and he just looks at me placidly and goes scritch scritch scritch.

JANUARY 30

It's great to have so many friends who had babies right around the time I did—even if it did make me bitter and resentful that they also got to have husbands and nurseries—because they all have extremely bad attitudes and sick senses of humor like me. It would be intolerable to call a friend, a new mother, when you were really feeling down and for her to say some weird aggressive shit like "Little Phil slept through the night yesterday, isn't that marvelous since he's only eight weeks old, and guess what, I'm already fitting back into my prepregnancy clothes." You'd really have no choice but to hope for disaster to rain down on such a person.

Yesterday Sam was horrible, whiny and wired and just in general the most worthless and irritating little person. By the late afternoon I was no longer stoned on the good news from *Mademoiselle*. In fact, I was quite depressed. On top of everything, I have developed a horrible new body odor. Maybe it's because sometimes there isn't enough time to give both me and the baby a bath, but when we went to the market I thought someone in line must have some terrible endocrine imbalance, and it turned out to be me. Pammy was busy all day and couldn't come over, and I just hated everything. So I called Donna, my novelist friend, whose son is five days younger than Sam. She'd been completely wasted and mental a few days earlier, and I'd managed to cheer her up: the more I think about it, the only reason various societies work is because we're not all depressed at the same time.

I said, "What are you doing?"

She said, "I'm just sitting here in my colic clothes, my spitty little nightgown, even though it's 4:00 in the afternoon, and I'm nursing little Elliott Abrams and eating my fourth doughnut."

"How do you feel?" I asked.

"I think I've been better," she said. We both started to laugh somewhat maniacally.

"I called for a reason," I said. "I need to know one thing. Are there any actual benefits to having an infant?"

There was a long silence.

"I don't think so," she said.

I asked, "Do you think having a husband makes it a lot easier?"

She said, "Oh, no, just the opposite. The only real advantage is that you get to have tantrums *and* someone to attack, which, actually, the more I think about it, does seem to relieve some of the pressure. You get to say things like 'I hate my life, I hate you, you're gone all day, this was your idea, my figure is ruined, you're a bad person, I hate you, and I hate listening to you floss every night. It makes me want to hang myself.' "

It doesn't look that funny on paper, but I laughed so hard that I could breathe again.

After I got off the phone with Donna, I called Pammy and asked her if I could yell all this stuff at her since she's the closest thing I have to a husband, and she said very nicely, "Oh, sure." So I did, I actually repeated everything Donna had said, even that I hated listening to her floss every night. She just listened silently; she was probably sorting laundry or giving her cat a flea dip while I ranted, and when I was done she asked if Sam and I wanted her to come up and watch the evening news with us, which, needless to say, we did.

Midnight

We're better, Sam is sleeping again. There were periods earlier when I got so stuck in the feelings of darkness that it felt like there were no safe places. I used to feel this a lot when I was a kid and a teenager. All those years I just wanted a family that was okay (except for those times when I thought maybe I'd settle for a police dog instead). And now I have one, a family that is okay, a family of me, a baby boy, and a cat, and the people I love most, who love me and are helping me to raise Sam. For instance, Peg brought over a whole bunch of meals today, one for tonight and some to freeze, and she took all of our laundry to the Laundromat and returned with it an hour and a half later, all of it clean and neatly folded. It felt like a small miracle to have enough clean clothes for four or five days. She said something so funny just before she left that I've repeated it four or five times over the phone and laughed all over again each time. She's such an entirely right-brain person—totally loving and intuitive, not in the least cerebral—

and she'd just read an article somewhere involving new revelations about Hitler's private life. She told me all about it while she was putting away our laundry, then shook her head angrily and said, "I've *had* it with Hitler."

JANUARY 31

I did a really dumb horrible thing late last night. I reread Raymond Carver's short story "A Small, Good Thing." I don't know why. It's like that old joke about the mighty lion who is holding a mouse upside down by its tail, dangling it back and forth in front of his eyes, telling it, "You are the weakest, most pitiful creature I've ever seen," and the mouse says, "I've been sick." That's me.

The story is about a man and woman who've ordered a cake from a bakery for their little son's birthday, but then the boy gets hit by a car and is in a coma. So they don't pick up the cake. The baker just thinks he's been stiffed and keeps calling and leaving mean messages, but then—oh, God, can you imagine—their little boy dies. And at the end of the story, the parents go to the bakery at dawn and against all odds end up eating bread and rolls with the baker.

I can't tell you the dread I felt as I read the story. I think there was something inside me that just felt we had to confront that awful possibility and wallow in it, instead of its being an evil shadow always walking behind us. But it was like having a rattlesnake in our little house, that's how huge the fear felt at first, that's how petrified I am of losing Sam. But then I suddenly realized that it was a Eucharist story, the breaking and sharing of bread, the dawn.

I tried to console myself, assuage my fear of children dying by saying we can't know what a soul's function on Earth is, but even so I couldn't stop crying. Everything felt so sad and precarious. I wished so desperately right then that I had a mate who would comfort me. It almost made me wish that I'd never had a baby. I read a line once in a book by Jonathan Nasaw about a place where children who were dying could stay with their parents. A hospice for children. I can hardly write these words. But there was a banner, tie-dyed, I think, over one of the rooms, or maybe over the entrance to the huge house, that said, "Turn off the light, the dawn is coming." I'll never forget that as long as I live. I stayed up very late, watching the baby sleep, trying to exhort him psychically to take deeper breaths. If I could have one wish, *just one crummy little wish*, it would be that Sam outlive me.

Megan told me today about the first time she baby-sat for an infant, a five-month-old, when she was about twelve and living in Kansas. The mother said there was cereal for the baby in the cupboard, but all Megan could find were Wheaties, so she assumed that's what the mother had in mind. She put them in a lot of milk, and waited until they were really soggy, and then tried to feed them to the baby. "And did he eat them?" I asked. "Well," she said, "he did as well as he could."

Sam had strained carrots again tonight. Big huge mess, carrots everywhere, all over the kitty who passed by at a bad time, on Sam's socks, in his hair, in my hair. I can see that things are going to begin deteriorating around here rather rapidly.

When he is asleep in his bassinet, the motions of his hands are as fluid and graceful as a ballerina's. They are like birds.

Tonight Sam and I took a friend of ours out to dinner, a young man in his late twenties who is badly strung out on booze and Methedrine but who is also a very sweet, bright guy. We went to McDonald's and got Quarter-Pounders and fries, and we were sitting in a booth with Sam on the table in his car seat, babbling. I was talking to the young man about recovery, which he was starved to hear about—I think it must have been like hearing about the sun during an ice age—and then Sam made a loud spluttering noise, so I said jokingly, "Shhh, honey, be patient, I know John plans to share his food with you," and I went on blithely with my recovery pitch, eating at the same time, not particularly paying attention. Then I looked up and noticed that my friend had torn off about a third of his burger and was holding it tentatively in his left hand, and he said to me, "Is that about right?" and I said, "Is what about right?" and he held out the small piece of hamburger and said with exasperation, "I just really don't have any idea how much he eats."

I mentioned this story to Pammy later, and she said, "Boy, scratch *him* off the baby-sitting list."

Sam loves the kitty more than anything else in life except for me and my breasts. On Valentine's Day we were in the kitchen and Sam was lying on his back on a blanket on the floor, and suddenly the cat came in and started rolling around on the floor near him, like some blowsy Swedish farm girl rolling around in the hay. Sam laughed for ten straight minutes. He sounded like a brook. The kitty would stop rolling for a moment, and Sam would kind of get a grip, catch his breath, and all but wipe his eyes like an old man, and then the kitty would fling herself into the rolling motion again and Sam would just go nuts. So I got down on all fours to be near him. I stared at him, listened to him laugh, and said out loud, "Now, *where* did you come from again?"

He loves his solid foods these days, plunging in with great vigor and pride. Every meal is like eating with Falstaff. His poops are like little meatballs now. Sometimes when I'm changing him, the little meatballs roll off the diaper and onto the floor, and I have to chase them down. It's sort of exhilarating—sort of sporting, or something. It makes me feel a little like Babe Zaharias.

Perhaps I am not getting out enough.

FEBRUARY 20

We are having a hard morning. I didn't sleep much last night; I woke up at 3:00 feeling discombobulated and afraid. I wish I had an armed husband or at least a dog. Everything would feel safer. I'm tired and wired and fat and feeling about as feminine and spiritual as the late great Divine. I am also totally bored. The kitty has been crying the blues all morning, and it is wearing badly on my nerves. I think I'll have her put to sleep this afternoon. Maybe that would cheer me up. At least it would be something to do.

Later

Sam has a marvelous new look of impatience. You see it cross his face when he first notices that he'd like to nurse. His brows furrow in a slightly sarcastic way, like he's about to ask, "Who the *hell* do you have to know to get a drink around here?"

He's so beautiful, so funny, so incredibly dear, and he smells like God. When Mom or Dudu have to hand him back over to me when they are about to leave, they lean into his airspace and sniff one last time, trying to memorize him, maybe storing a little hit for later.

We all lean into him, soaking him up. It's like he's giving

off a huge amount of energy because he hasn't had to start putting up a lot of barriers around it to protect himself. He hasn't had to start channeling it into managing the world and everybody's emotions around him, so he's a pure burning furnace of the stuff. This is my theory, anyway, that he radiates it; it's probably affecting us all like a spray of negative ions, like being in a long hot shower or at the seashore.

For instance, I notice that the kitty, who, like all cats, is a heat freak, stands right next to him all the time. She basks in him. He's her own private tanning salon. When he falls asleep, she waits patiently for a moment and then begins to butt him with her head, as if it's 2:00 in the morning and the bar has just shut down and she wasn't ready to go.

He's sleeping now, loudly, like a drunken baby angel in a cartoon.

It's great to feel better, to be back in the saddle again. And it's so hard to let chaos swirl around without needing to manage or understand it. It's so hard to get quiet enough, free enough of the bondage of self, to hear the voice in the whirlwind that Job heard. There's always so much shouting going on in here. It's a cacophony of sounds from my childhood— parents and relatives and teachers and preachers and voices distilled into what has become my conscience. But I don't think the still small voice is my conscience. Maybe it's God, maybe it's the true unique essential me—and maybe those are the same thing. It's so hard to hear it though, and sometimes when I think I hear something in my own true voice, I'm so nuts that I'm not sure if it's me or someone pretending to be me. It seems like when it's really you, the voice doesn't even have to talk.

My friend Larry, the scholarly one who has HIV, says it's important to remember that God is present in many, many ways in the world if you're just looking. You don't have to go to the cathedral or the temple or the sacred grove to find calmness and faith. Sometimes we just can't quiet the mind— it's like some crazy riled-up two-year-old who can't get to sleep—but we can find our own steadiness in the middle of that and see it as some form of God. We can notice all the chaos and voices and know that they are one aspect of the mind but that they are not our *nature*. Our true nature is more like Sam's, lovely and alert and peaceful and entranced.

Sam is a happy person. He has this little Yoda smile. He is a poem. It seems like he's turning out okay. It's all these people who love him so much and take care of us both. Maybe it also helps that there is no angry dad stomping around. But that always hurts so much to think about, because it would also be great to have a kind and funny dad here with us, hanging out, maybe even helping a little. I take a long deep breath.

Sam's such a gift. Dudu and Rex love him passionately, would kidnap him and raise him on their own if they thought they could get away with it. And my mom and her twin sister, who used to bicker a lot more, take him every Thursday for most of the afternoon so I can either see my therapist or go to a matinee with Pammy. They sit around beaming at one another, like Christian Scientists or something. It's like Sam opened this window for us, and all this grace flooded in.

Little by little I think I'm letting go of believing that I'm in charge, that I'm God's assistant football coach. It's so incredibly hard to let go of one's passion for control. It seems like if you stop managing and controlling, everything will spin off into total pandemonium and it will be all your fault.

FEBRUARY 22

Sam looks exactly like the baby pictures of my dad in Tokyo. Watching him sleep, I sometimes bite my lip.

My gay friend Jane, who, like me, used to drink a little bit more than was perhaps good for her, said on the winter solstice this year that for her, being a pagan, the solstice is not just about the darkest night of the year but also about the darkest night of the soul. She and her goddess-worshiping friends celebrate this because the seeds of new growth lie in this darkness and develop in the winter to bloom in the spring. I said, What do you pagan homos do at your midnight celebrations—put a bunch of dogs in wicker baskets and push them off cliffs, with Holly Near playing on a nearby boom box? And she looked over at my big Italian crucifix on the kitchen wall, at the thorns, at the bloody wound, the nails through his palms, and then she turned to me with a look of such amused condescension that all I could do was laugh. As soon as she left, though, I went and stared at the crucifix for a long time and breathed it in. I *believe* in it, and it's so nuts. How did some fabulously cerebral and black-humored cynic like myself come to fall for all that Christian lunacy, to see the cross not as an end but a beginning, to believe as much as I believe in gravity or in the size of space that Jesus paid a debt he didn't owe because we had a debt we couldn't pay? It, my faith, is a great mystery. It has all the people close to me shaking their heads. It has *me* shaking my head. But I have a photograph on my wall of this ancient crucifix at a church over in Corte Madera, a tall splintering wooden Christ with his arms blown off in some war, under which someone long ago wrote, "Jesus has no arms but ours to do his work and to show his love," and every time I read that, I always end up thinking that these are the only operating instructions I will ever need.

. . .

The cross, though: was it Lenny Bruce who said that if Jesus had been killed in modern times, we Christians would all go around wearing little electric chairs on chains around our necks?

FEBRUARY 23

Sam can sit up by himself now without having to be propped up with pillows. I used to surround him entirely with pillows so he could sit around without my having to hold him. Donna used to call it Fort Samuel, and she used to tell him that Fort Samuel was a state of mind. But now he can sit up by himself. Everything is going by so quickly. You know how when you're at the library, and you get one of those reels of tape that hold two weeks' worth of newspapers, and you put the reel on and then wind it forward really fast to the date you're looking for, but you see every day pass by for about half a minute? That's what it feels like to me now.

Sam, who was so recently larval and incompetent, is almost crawling. He moved backwards half a foot tonight. I feel that these are his first steps out of the present. He used to trip out only on whatever was within his narrow vision and grasp, but now he sees something a few feet away and he gets this glinty Donald Trump look in his eyes, like in the old cartoons where someone gets a greedy brainstorm, blinks, and we hear the sound of a cash register and see the dollar signs in his eyes.

He's crawling inexorably away from the now. He's crawling toward anticipated pleasures. Soon there will be scheming and manipulation, a dedication to certain outcomes, to attaining certain things and storing them for later. I'm trying so hard to learn to live in the now, to bring my mind back to the present, while Sam is learning to anticipate and plan, to want things that are far away.

It's funny to watch a baby crawl backwards because it's something you grow out of—after a while you're only sup-posed to go forward. I think this is a part of the voice that says constantly, Fix, fix, fix; do, do, do—the part of us that believes there is always something to fix or to do. It is so fucking bizarre and excruciating just to be. Just to be still. I mean, except when I'm in church or nursing Sam, nothing can make me more frantic than sitting and trying to just *be*. Have you ever tried meditating? For me it's about as pleasant as coming down off cocaine. My mind becomes like this badly abused lab rat, turning in on itself after one too many bouts with Methe-drine and electroshock and immersions into ice water, and I can't get into some fantasizing and mind-fucking fast enough.

Anyway, I watch Sam be a baby and crawl backwards, and it's such an alien concept because it seems so natural to think that all the action is forward. Actually, backwards is just as rich as forward if you can appreciate the circle instead of the direction.

FEBRUARY 24

Pammy has gone to Morocco for a month. I am completely distraught. I find I've been sort of scared since she left, like she was somehow keeping us safe. I'm watching Sam sleep a lot, to make sure he's okay. It's hard to believe how shallowly babies breathe when they're sleeping. They're like plants.

FEBRUARY 27

I was a mess all morning. Maybe my hormones are raging, maybe that's what the craziness was all about. Something is really off. Part of me wants my body back, wants to stop being a moo-cow, and part of me thinks about nursing him through kindergarten. I know a woman who nursed her daughter until the girl was almost four, and of course we all went around thinking that it was a bit much, too *Last Emperor* for *our* blood. But now when Sam and I are nursing, it crosses my mind that I will never ever be willing to give this up. It'll be okay, I think to myself, we can get it to work, I'll follow him to college but I'll stay *totally* out of the way. . . .

This the easiest, purest communication I've ever known.

MARCH 2

He's six months old now, the most gorgeous, alert baby you ever saw in your life. Everyone says so. Maybe they just say so because I'm so goddamn tired and mentally ill so often. I had two days of bad depression this week. Peg came to cook for us and baby-sat so I could go hang out with a bunch of other recovering alkies. They were funny; it helped to be with them. But still I would love, *love* to check out sometimes, especially when I feel like I did yesterday and the day before. The weather sucked, gray and heavy and damp and dark. I felt like I was really hurt somehow, in a deep way. I can't explain it. And there was nothing to do but feel it and maybe talk about it a little with friends. Pictures of glasses of wine kept crossing my mind, and I thought about how great a few hundred lines of cocaine would feel. I kept remembering that old joke about how when a normal person's car breaks down, she calls a tow truck; when an addict's car breaks down, she calls her dealer.

It finally occurred to me the next morning to call my therapist, and we talked for five minutes. That helped a little, maybe even more than a little. I was really aware when I called her that I wanted a fix, that I couldn't stand the feelings of exhaustion and loneliness and fear and anger. When I mentioned this to her, she reminded me of a story that I had once told *her.* It was something that M. F. K. Fisher wrote about in one of her books, of having a friend over for tea one day. The friend noticed out the kitchen window that Mary Frances's cat was lying in a big mud puddle. Mary Frances said that it was hurt and trying to take care of itself, but the friend asked, Then shouldn't we take it to the vet? Mary Frances said no, absolutely not, that if she did, the cat would die, that the cat knew exactly and intuitively what to do, knew that only time and lying in the mud would heal her. A few days later the cat was okay again.

That's how I felt after my dad died. I had to shut down almost entirely and just lie in the mud for months. I felt that the world was no longer safe if my young handsome lively father could be so suddenly dead. It felt like it was a shooting gallery out there. And I felt like my heart had been so thoroughly and irreparably broken that there could be no real joy again, that at best there might eventually be a little contentment. Everyone wanted me to get help and rejoin life, pick up the pieces and move on, and I tried to, I wanted to, but I just had to lie in the mud with my arms wrapped around myself, eyes closed, grieving, until I didn't have to anymore. And then over time I became more or less okay: I did feel joy again, and I feel it now sometimes bigger than I ever thought possible. It's so big inside me now with Sam that it's like a secret that might make me burst, like when you're in love.

MARCH 3

Sam now sleeps in our little tiny bedroom at the far end of the apartment in a beautiful crib that someone has lent us. God, he's so grown up. It goes so crazily fast that it's no wonder we're all just a little bit edgy. One day you're six months old and learning to crawl backwards, and then about ten hours later you look like Alan Cranston. Have you seen him lately? He was a great senator, a great man, and I'm sorry bad things are happening to him, but still I've got to say that he looks absolutely cadaverous. He can't weigh more than about 105. I've got *pantyhose* that weigh more than he does.

Sam's a good sleeper for the most part. I put him facedown in his crib, and he does a few baby push-ups. It's this very manly little ritual he has. He turns to look joyfully at me, like it's great that we've simply moved the party from the living room to the bedroom, but then he understands that I am going to turn off the light and leave him, and this look of terror and total betrayal crosses his face. *Total* betrayal; basset hound death. His lips tremble, and he weeps for a moment in this pitiful little-guy way. Then he goes to sleep, just like that.

I start to think about the millions of things I could do around the house or at my desk, and I decide on just one thing that could really make a difference in the quality of our life, and then I usually end up thinking, Gee, that sounds like a lot of work for a woman who hasn't brushed her teeth in three days.

MARCH 4

Sam's got this fabulous little fake cough now. The advice nurse at Kaiser said lots of babies get little coughs from all the teething drool, but I would swear he's just doing it because he can, like that Eddie Murphy routine where he says, "You know why male dogs lie around all day licking their balls? Because they *can*. If I could do that, I'd never leave the house. . . ." Sam will look at me suddenly with great concern and go, Cough cough cough, quiet and tragic, and then look at me expectantly, and I'll say, "Oh, Sam, honey, that's an *awful* cough," and he looks terribly pleased. Then his eyes grow wide again, and he goes, Cough cough cough.

His eyes are very dark and huge. Most of his body is taken up with these eyes.

My friends and I did a food review again after all these months. I loved being out with my gang again—Peg, Leroy, Bill, and Emmy—and for the first couple of hours I loved being away from Sam. I felt once again like Zorba the Greek, with my arms stretched out to the sky, dancing to balalaika music. Everyone was very funny. Then all of a sudden I felt this psychotic need to be with Sam again—the jungle drums started beating, and I could hardly take in what anyone was saying. I couldn't get home fast enough—my breasts were absolutely bursting with milk—and I rushed to the crib and woke Sam up, and he gave me this bewildered, derisive look, like "Don't you have any *friends?*"

Maybe he's not really capable of loving me per se. I think maybe I can only love or understand God in that same baby way. I don't know. Donna says that when our babies see us, they say, Oh, good, the chuck wagon's here again.

MARCH 5

I was reading something the other day and came upon the word *bastard*, as in illegitimate, and it actually crossed my mind for the first time that Sam is illegitimate. Maybe I've lost too much ground over the last year and a half, but I swear it hadn't occurred to me before. I mulled it over for a few moments, saw that in a legal sense the word maybe did apply, but then I thought, Nah.

We have a new comedy routine we do to amuse our friends. It's called Crane Operator. I am the crane operator, and he is the crane—I carry him suspended about a foot off the floor, motoring over toward, say, an orange, making engine sounds the whole time, and then when we're directly over the orange, I lower him until he can slide his hands under it and somehow get a grip on it. Then I raise him, holding the orange, and our friends clap.

They are a simple people.

MARCH 6

He splashes in the sink now while taking his bath, slaps the water and squeals, like some yahoo from *Deliverance*.

When he thinks I've left, he cries. When he thinks Megan's left, he cries. When he sees that we are still here, relief pours over his face and his entire body, like one of those old nudie pens where you turn it upside down to get the swimsuit to pour back over the woman.

Everything feels funny and not real. It's that old familiar feeling of having a dental X-ray apron on my chest. I keep thinking of these lines I have taped to my wall that someone once sent in a letter; they're from Rilke's *Sonnets to Orpheus*:

And if the earth has forgotten you
Say to the still earth: I am flowing.
To the rushing waters say: I am.

Sam seems like a really happy baby. I don't know why I'm so sad.

MARCH 16

I wish I felt more like writing. I don't particularly feel like I have anything to say these days. I feel like the propulsion is missing. All that emptiness and desire and craving and feeling and need to achieve used to keep me at the typewriter. Now there's me and Sam, and it feels like there's not any steam in my pressure cooker. Whenever I teach, I tell my students about that line of Doctorow's, that when you're writing a novel, it's like driving in a tulle fog: you can only see about as far as the headlights, but that's enough; it's as far as you have to see. And I tell them that this probably applies to real life, too. But right now I feel like I'm just sitting in the car with Sam, not really going anywhere, just getting to know each other, both of us looking out through the window at what passes by, and then at each other again.

The slow pace and all this rumination wear me down and bore me and make me desperately want a hit of something, of anything. Adrenaline, say, or a man to fantasize about or have drama with, or some big professional pressure, like a deadline I'm just barely going to be able to make. I want to check out. I do not want to be in the here and now with God and myself and all that shit. I know that this is where all the real blessings and payoffs are, that there is a good reason they call the now "the present." I want to learn to live in the now, I want to learn to breathe my way into it and hang out there more and more and experience life in all its richness and realness. But I want to do it later, like maybe sometime early next week. Right now I want a rush.

Last year when I was obsessing over this married man whom I adore and who adores me and with whom I was trying to avoid having an affair, I talked about it with this older lesbian, a recovering alcoholic and addict. I was talking about how often I wanted to call him, and how, when we saw each other, I wanted to drop these erotically charged bombs into the conversation, and how high I'd get off all the adrenaline, and how it felt like it validated my parking ticket because he was so luscious and powerful. And the lesbian said, really nicely, "Yeah, yeah, I get it, I've done it. But I think each step of the way you gotta ask yourself, Do I want the *hit* or do I want the serenity?"

It seemed one of the most profound things I'd ever heard,

and it's helped me a hundred times since—with food, men, etc.—but at the time, to the lesbian, and right now, to myself, I said, Honey, I want the *hit.*

Sam can get up on all fours now, but he can't actually move that way. He drags himself from place to place, though. It's a little like *My Left Foot* around here these days.

He often makes a beautiful pealing shriek of pleasure and surprise.

At church, during the "prayers of the people," members of the congregation share these incredibly sad stories of their own lives and the lives of friends who need help. They ask that we pray for their families, and for kinder leaders, and for the homeless, and people with AIDS, and people in other countries in crises of starvation or war. The whole time, Sam sits there making joyful loud farting noises with his mouth. He sounds like a human whoopee cushion. I clap my hand over his mouth, but he just makes the loud farting noises directly into my hand. And they still call him their baby. "Oh, that's *our* baby, sugar, huh? That's *our* baby."

All of his sounds bring him such joy. He's learning the range of his voice, learning to play it like a musical instrument.

M A R C H   2 0

He'll be seven months old in nine days. He's really scooting around like mad now, doing some real distances but still not crawling on his hands and knees. Sometimes he stops and lifts his arms and legs and appears to be swimming in a thrashing kind of way. Megan and I were watching him do this today, and Megan said to him, with a real mixture of sympathy and encouragement, "Gee, honey, if you were in the water, you'd be there by now."

I am really trying to trust God, to believe in the tenderness of a God who cares even about a bruised reed, or a hurt bird, and certainly about this happy little baby. I feel the presence of that tenderness in the people who love Sam and me, who bring us groceries and help us keep our spirits up. But I'm still fucked up and feeling off my feed so much of the time. I know the solution is to slow down, and breathe, and learn to pay attention. My friend Bonnie's kids went to a kindergarten with a sign over the front door that said, "Start out slow, and taper off." It's so easy and natural to race around too much, letting days pass in a whirl of being busy and mildly irritated, getting fixed on solutions to things that turn out to have been just farts in the windstorm. Our culture encourages this kind of behavior. That's why we call it the rat race. Some days I get stoned on the pace, but today it is making me incredibly sad. That's probably a healthy sign. Maybe I'll learn to slow down and breathe in time for it to help Sam. Peg's friends over in AA say that the willingness comes from the pain, by which they mean the willingness to change; in other words, people don't get sober when they are still having fun drinking. Today I feel like one old rat who wants to get off the exercise wheel.

Maybe if I can learn to breathe and go slower, I can somehow help Sam be spared some of the craziness I had in my life, all that chasing down of these things that I thought would make me okay or would prove that I was okay. A lot of it, looking back, was metaphorically the serpent in the garden. I like that line of Kazantzakis's in *The Last Temptation of Christ* when he says, "The doors of heaven and hell are adjacent and identical; both green, both beautiful."

Still, you know what the name Samuel means? It means "God has heard," like God heard me, heard my heart, and gave me the one thing that's ever worked in my entire life, someone to love.

MARCH 24

I'm just feeling stressed to the nu-nu's today, very tired and unable to keep the house and our life together. It is clear to me that we need a breadwinner. Also, servants. I opened the fridge to make us some lunch and could instantly smell that something was suffering in there, but I did not have the psychic energy to deal with it. I don't think I will tomorrow, either. I think the easiest thing would just be to move.

He moves so fast these days, like a lizard. He's babbling with great incoherent animation. He gets on all fours and rocks, like he's about to take off, like Edwin Moses in the starting block. His new thing is that he likes to stick his fingers in your mouth and examine your teeth. He does it every time we nurse. Maybe he wants to be a periodontist when he grows up. It's a little disconcerting. He'll stare at my mouth for a minute when he's lying in my arms, and then reach in with these tiny monkey fingers and go tooth by tooth, checking each one for problems. Next he's going to start picking cooties out of my hair. When Sam is doing my teeth, I sit there basking in our monkey lives.

I really felt like smoking today. It's been almost four years. It would be the answer to a lot of my problems—weight control and stress management, for instance. A friend of mine with a difficult baby Sam's age—we call her "little Evita"—started smoking again a few months ago, and she's become very thin and self-possessed. Of course, she smells like Nagasaki, but if you're thin, who cares? I hear that practically all Michelle Pfeiffer does is smoke and go bowling. I rest my case.

Sam's got this new maturity all of a sudden. Part of it is about being so terribly pleased with himself. He is so fast and physically adept that he can hardly contain himself. I'm cheering him on and blown away by each new skill, but at the same time the corners of my mouth turn down, like a mime's.

I remember when he was always sort of placidly stoned and incompetent, like this puzzled little baby I saw in L.A. when I was pregnant. I could not take my eyes off her. We were staring at each other in a sidewalk café in the Palisades, in similar states of burnout, neither of us blinking very much, and all I could think of was a baby that Ram Dass described in a book I read years ago; he believed this baby to be a very old lama, someone who had been incarnated tens of thousands of times, a very old soul who was born this time as a baby in the Bronx, one of those very stoned-looking babies who are wondering what on earth they are doing here and who want to bless everybody but can't get it to work.

That's exactly how Sam seemed a lot of the time when he was an infant. Maybe all infants have that look. But now, he's *happening.* Steve thinks he is finally beginning to enjoy his stay here, and not only that but he may want to be one of us when he grows up. There's definitely a sense that he's the new man at the company and is now ready to start working his way up the ladder.

MARCH 25

He's definitely got his daddy's thick, straight hair, and, God, am I grateful for that. It means he won't have to deal with hat hair as he goes through life. This morning as we were racing around, I was trying to get us both fed and ready for church, and I had *total* hat hair. When you have extremely curly hair, it is always getting mashed down into weird patterns, like grass that's been flattened. You get it when you wear hats, and you get it when you sleep. In extreme cases, you wake up looking like a horse has been grazing on one side of your head all night. I know hat hair is not as bad as having, say, Lou Gehrig's disease, but still I'm glad that Sam will be spared.

On the day I was born, I think God reached down and said, "Baby girl Annie, I am going to give you a good brain and some artistic talent and a sense of humor, but I'm also going to give you low self-esteem and hat hair, because I want you to fight your way back to me."

Bonnie, whose three daughters are half black, has a poster of Jesus with fluffy, nappy hair, just like her children's, just like mine.

Church was especially sweet this morning. Of course, it goes without saying that the more quiet and sacred any occasion, the more you can count on Sam having terrible flatulence. Today, during the period of silent confession, it was like machine-gun fire. I think it may be another guy thing. I don't think girl babies do this. Plus he continues to make loud farting noises with his mouth, so it's like bringing a wiseacre drunk or a jackhammer to church. It's hard to express how loud this sixteen-pound baby can be. I stood up during the "prayers of the people" to say how happy and relieved I felt to be there. Sam started farting again, not with his mouth, and I just stood there holding him, crying, and trying to talk about God and about how crazy my past was and how mostly beautiful my life is now. Through my tears, every time he farted I'd start to laugh, and I thought later that it must be music to God's ears—someone trying to voice her gratitude while she laughs and cries and her big-eyed baby farts.

There was this East Indian Jesuit named Tony de Mello who used to tell this story about disciples gathered around their master, asking him endless questions about God. And the master said that anything we say about God is just words, because God is unknowable. One disciple asked, "Then why do you speak of him at all?" and the master replied, "Why does the bird sing?" She sings not because she has a statement but because she has a song.

MARCH 26

Today he rode in a shopping cart for the first time. He was blissed out, stoned, bug-eyed. He looked like Buckwheat. He passed out almost immediately after we got back into the car. The excitement must have been too much for him. His eyes rolled back in his head as he fell asleep, but this time I didn't slap him or try to wake him. I finally remembered what our Lamaze teacher had told Pammy and me—that you never *ever* wake up your secondborn, so try to remember that when you are about to wake up your first.

It will be interesting to see if he remembers Pammy. She will be home in a few days. I'm sure he will. She was one of the first two people to hold him after his arrival here on the outside. She's been his second mother. He might feel shy at first, though, because he's a little shy at first with everyone but me. When I come home to him, he just goes ape-shit, like he'd given me up for dead. It's like George Carlin's impersonation of a dog—frantic and breathless with relief that his human has come back, going, "Oh, Jesus God, I'm so glad you're back, I was going out of my mind, I was beside myself, I didn't think I could last another fifteen minutes," and his human says, "I just came back to get my *hat*, for Chrissakes." That's exactly how Sam is.

He scoots joyfully all over but still doesn't move with his stomach off the floor; i.e., he does not officially crawl. He's like a salamander moving through the mud.

Today a friend with a little baby Sam's age called, and in the beginning of the conversation, her baby was cooing and peeping quietly. All of a sudden I heard the baby begin to babble animatedly, and then she burst into tears. My friend comforted her for a moment, and the baby was quiet again. "What on earth was that all about?" I asked. My friend said, "Oh, the great god Dad just came into the room and then left, and now she's frustrated." I felt a flush of many feelings all at once— longing, jealousy, sorrow beyond words that Sam doesn't have a daddy. He will grieve over the years, and there is nothing I can do or say that will change the fact that his father chooses not to be his father. I can't give him a dad, I can't give him a nuclear family. All I can do is to give him what I have, some absolutely wonderful men in our lives who loved him before he was born, who over the years will play with him, read and fish and walk with him, make him laugh and throw him up in the air until he is too big, men who will be his uncles and brothers and friends, and I have to believe that this will be a great consolation.

MARCH 27

I was secretly infatuated with a man for a few days this week, and it was just awful, like bad drugs. His packaging was nearly perfect. He's tall, nice-looking, with lots of money and a degree from Stanford, but most of all he's very funny, definitely a snappy piece of cheese. He called last night, and when I heard his voice, I felt on the verge of hyperventilating. I had to force myself to calm down so that I wouldn't start wheezing. My back lit up, and there was a burning sensation in my neck. I was hanging on everything he said so I could micromanage each word and inflection, looking for a hidden meaning. On the inside I felt like the George Carlin dog, but I played it cool and was as funny as I've been in a long time. We talked for half an hour and didn't make a date. We said we would talk again soon. I got off the phone and fantasized for a while about having this tender romantic sex with him. Then I called a woman who went out with him a few years ago and discovered the two most damaging things I can know about a man: one, he voted for both Bush and Reagan, and two, he was very very reluctant to give head. Now maybe on a really bad night I would let one of these things go by, but I tell you, if his head wouldn't go south of my waist and he was up there talking with passion about the thousand points of light, I'd crack. It would be like "Hey, thanks for stopping by, pal, but the thousand points of light are in my pussy." I don't want to feel like I have to negotiate the SALT talks just to get a little oral sex. The right guy will love nothing more.

Maybe I'm not well enough to have sex at all right now. I thought I was, but it all sounds sort of disgusting the more I think about it. Right now I secretly want everyone to be pristine and beautiful, like a summer lake, instead of being real, with all those little pimples and weird vein activity. Plus, with this latest crush, the last thing I'd want is to have to worry about a boyfriend sidling up to Sam in the middle of the night and whispering right-wing propaganda into his baby ears, stuff about supply-side economics and welfare cheats. So I've been restored to sanity.

It would be one thing if I could leap into a disastrous romance and it would be just me who would suffer, but I can't afford to get lost because Sam doesn't have anyone else to fall back on. And *I* don't have anyone else to fall back on, come to think of it. I can afford to wait for a good one, not get derailed by some total fixer-upper. Once my agent Abby said that if we're not careful, we'll spend our whole lives blowing on sparks and trying to turn them into embers, when all along they were sparks that should never have been ignited. In that capacity, I've looked like Neptune, cheeks filled with wind, blowing on the sea.

It gives me the chill to think about beginning a new relationship, even though of course I would love to find a man to love and grow old with. You see these seemingly perfect couples and feel like the kid with her nose pressed against the window of the candy store, but then you get to know them and learn all the ratty underbelly stuff about them, that they are cold to one another, or sarcastic, or unfaithful. I have loved men so much and am so afraid of what they will do to me. On bad days, I think straight white men are so poorly wired, so emotionally unenlightened and unconscious that you must approach each one as if he were some weird cross between a white supremacist and an incredibly depressing T. S. Eliot poem. I know they were very badly hurt and misled, but so was I, and I chose and am choosing to get well. I am sorry for how they were raised and for all the fears about their thinning hair and little penises, but I mean, bore me fucking later, try having been raised female in this culture. Most men shut down like sea anemones or bank vaults the moment things get too intimate or too dicey. I lived with a man who when he had hurt me enough—not that he meant to, but he always did—he would cry with fear that he would end up old and alone, never having really lived. And then I'd have to comfort him and nurse him back to health because he was so sad and I loved him so much, and I'd help him be able to reconnect with me again, but then two or three weeks later I'd look up and see that cold flat reptilian look in his eyes again. I am too old and tired and too well to do this anymore. Maybe.

I heard this friend of mine named James, who is really a great guy in a lot of ways, smart and reasonably sensitive, telling another friend of ours the other day about this woman he has fallen deeply in love with. He was describing how totally cool she is, intelligent and sensitive and caring, and then he says quite earnestly—and I am not making this up—that she could suck a bowling ball through a garden hose. I tried to explain to James that if you really love someone, you don't go around telling people that she can suck a bowling ball through a rubber hose. You just don't. But he didn't get it at all. We had a small fight, and my impression is that he came away thinking that it was still okay to say it, just not if there were a bunch of hostile feminists around. God, we are an interesting species.

I miss Pammy so much today. It was horrible of her to go away, and I'll never forgive her. I will find someone new. There are plenty of other fish in the sea, women who would rejoice in being my best friend. I will tell people terrible things about her, make up stories about her past, tell everyone I know that she can suck a bowling ball through a garden hose.

March 28

One thing about Sam, one thing about having a baby, is that each step of the way you simply cannot imagine loving him any more than you already do, because you are bursting with love, loving as much as you are humanly capable of—and then you do, you love him even more.

He's figuring out little concepts all the time these days, like that if something falls out of his hands, it is not instantly vaporized but just might be found somewhere on the floor. Even a week ago Sam was like some rich guy who drops some change and doesn't even give it a second glance, but now when he drops something, he slowly cranes his neck and peers downward, as if the thing fell to the floor of a canyon.

MARCH 29

Today is his seven-month birthday, and he crawled. He crawls. He's a crawling guy now. He crawls in this lumbering, barrel-chested way, like a Komodo dragon. I saw glee and smugness and danger in his face today, as if he had just been handed the keys to the car.

MARCH 31

He's been sitting up by himself for a long time now, no longer needing to be surrounded by pillows, but I can see that he remains Fort Samuel, because as Donna keeps reminding me, Fort Samuel is simply a state of mind. Also, I finally set up the playpen the people from my church gave me. At first I thought we'd started it too late, because he'd only last a few minutes before he'd look completely bereft and forsaken and dying, like when the Bushman in *The Gods Must Be Crazy* was in that jail cell. If I didn't pick him up right away, he'd start to cry. But we have had playpen practice for a little while twice a day, and today he sat in it for twenty minutes, playing with his toys and babbling.

APRIL 3

Uncle Steve came by just in time for playpen practice, which Steve immediately dubbed Office Hours. "Time for your office hours, honey," he said, popping him into the playpen, and Sam entertained himself with his toys for quite a while, throwing things, banging toys together, putting smaller toys inside of bigger ones. I simply could not believe my eyes. Comparing this to even a month ago, let alone six, when he couldn't do anything but nurse and poop, when he couldn't hold his head up, focus, or chew, I felt like this was a miraculous apparition, one I would hold up against Bernadette seeing the Virgin in the grotto near Lourdes.

APRIL 4

Pammy is back, looking fantastic, missing Sam terribly and me just a little. Sam did not seem to remember her at first and then was all over her like a cheap suit. She held him for half an hour and let him do his periodontal work on her teeth and gums almost the whole time. "Oh, dear," she said, "does he do my nose next?"

Here's the difference in our personalities. Last night I put a brand-new bottle of maple syrup on the top shelf of the cupboard, and I laid it on its side because it was too tall to fit standing up, but because of brain waste I forgot to push the spout closed. So this morning the entire contents had dripped down all three shelves' worth of cups and plates and packages of food. It took an hour to clean up (thank God for the playpen), and my head was filled with visions of ants, trillions of ants, ants everywhere, marching up the street in phalanxes, dropping by parachute, brought in on stretchers. But Pammy walked into the kitchen and said, like the little kid who finds his closet full of horse shit and thinks it means his parents bought him a pony, "Oh, it just smells so wonderful in here now—like the International House of Pancakes."

I said, "I don't know what I see in you sometimes."

APRIL 5

Something has happened that is not possible. Pammy found a lump in her breast today.

APRIL 6

Just like that. Boom. Can you imagine? Just like that. I feel a dread like hearing sirens late at night, like I did with my dad. I know it's bad. There's no doubt in my mind.

APRIL 8

Today is my dad's birthday. He would have been sixty-seven. He's been dead eleven years. I could smash out every window in my house. Pammy and I went to a matinee today and overate. My mother and Aunt Pat watched the baby. What are you going to do? Life has got to be bigger than death, and love has got to be bigger than fear or this is all a total bust and we are all just going tourist class.

APRIL 9

Bad mammogram. Bad news. She had a biopsy today. The doctor is worried. Pammy is okay but very sad. When I nurse Sam, my tears stream down over him.

APRIL 10

It's my birthday today. I'm thirty-six. I once wrote a book where a little boy named Joe woke up one morning on his birthday. I think he was eight or nine, and his parents weren't getting along at all that day, and he went out into the garden, found his cat, and whispered to her, "It's my birthday today."

A PRIL 17

Oh, God. Things are crappy here. Pammy had two malignant lumps removed from her right breast yesterday and will have her lymph nodes removed on Monday. One of the lumps is a more aggressive form of cancer, the other is not so bad. Life is full of unexploded land mines, and she seems to have stepped on one. I don't know what to make of this.

Her husband was gone last weekend, so she came over and we watched *Wings of Desire,* that German movie where two angels, who look like a couple of homely middle-aged men, are hanging around Berlin. Only children can see them. They keep helping hopeless people who want to give up on life, by touching or laying their heads down compassionately on the sad person's shoulders. Suddenly the sad person will look around and start to have the vaguest sense of hope. For instance, there's a youngish man on the bus in one scene, and we hear his despairing thoughts, wondering what it's all about because it hurts so much, and then we see—although he can't—that one of the angels has sat down beside him. After listening to the man's thoughts for a moment, the angel tenderly puts his head on the man's shoulder, and we hear the man's thoughts change, not to ebullience, but to the very beginnings of hope. And Pammy, who doesn't really believe in

God, has called a few times since then to say she's gone into deep despair and terror and then felt someone put his head near hers.

She comes over a lot to play with us, and she is still, as our old mutual friend Neshama puts it, incandescently beautiful.

APRIL 20

I need to try and focus on Sam for a few days. Otherwise I am growing too sad. Sam is scooting and crawling and saying Dada. That warms the very cockles of my heart. He is very loud, very assertive. He pulled himself into a standing position the other night. He's so mobile now, and I am so tired. I feel like I'm breaking my motherly balls trying to keep him safe. Sometimes he's the Dalai Lama, and sometimes he's like a cross between a bad boyfriend and a high-strung puppy. And it never matters what my needs are. He never says, "Hey, babe, you've been working too hard—why don't you take a couple of hours off? I'll just lie here and read."

MAY I

Sam can now routinely pull himself up into a standing position. I feel that my life as I have known it is over. Nap time is now impossible because he ends up standing in his crib, grasping and shaking the slats like someone in an old James Cagney prison movie, shouting idle threats. Thank God for Megan. Now I can leave for a walk when this craziness starts up. I don't know why I'm so surprised that things have become so loud. Did I think that babies would be entertained all the time just playing with themselves, going, "Wow, ten toes! One, two, three—wow! Four, five, six, seven . . ."?

Lots of the other babies Sam's age have been crawling for months. Their moms say, "Oh, Joshua was one of those babies who couldn't wait to crawl," and their tone suggests that this is some positive reflection on his moral character. I always want to say, Yeah, but your kid's a spoiled little no-neck monster and your husband is a *total dork*. But hey—congratulations on the crawling!

I'm still nursing full-time, day and night. Donna says to William, whenever she whips out a breast to nurse him, "Hungry, honey? Is that it? Because you *know* we never close here at Chez Mommy. . . ." I call myself Mama with Sam, as opposed to Mommy, whenever I refer to myself in the third person. It's so Elvis, so Jimmy Carter.

He's so goddamn beautiful it breaks my heart. Maybe I could handle his beauty if Pammy weren't sick. I still have a lot of anxieties about fucking him up with my selfishness or because I cling too tightly to him. In his first days here, I'd think, Well, he won't ever be able to get into college because I don't flash black-and-white images at him so he can develop his vision. Now I look at how clingy and selfish I am, and how much I cry since Pammy got sick, and I worry that it's wrecking him, and he'll end up killing people and burying them in his basement and getting his photograph taken with Rosalynn Carter, like all those whacked-out serial killers in the late seventies—John Gacy, Jim Jones, etc. I asked Donna if she worries that William will end up at the top of a tower shooting at people when he grows up, and she said, "Nah, Jews don't shoot people. We just noodge them to death."

Later in the Afternoon

Pammy's cancer is bad; she just called. It's in six of her lymph nodes but not in her bones. We are crazy and bewildered. It's a nightmare. She seems sort of all right with it, but maybe she's in shock. I told her what my friend Elizabeth once told her friend Rae, "I'll give you one of anything I have two of—kidneys, lungs, you name it." Pammy said thank you, because she knows I mean it. The jungle drums are beating loudly tonight.

MAY 2

All day Pammy has been asking me to do favors for her—to please tie a scarf in my hair, "because I like how you look that way," or to cook her a quesadilla. Then she says that I *have* to do whatever she asks because it's her last wish. This is all that gallows humor, all that hard laughter, just like when my dad was sick. I said, "If you die, can I have all your shoes?" And she said sure, but she wears a size seven, and I wear a seven and a half, but then she added, really nicely, "I'll start buying bigger shoes."

She can't handle holding Sam right now, although at the same time it's just about her greatest solace. It's the one thing that makes her cry. She and I are both afraid she won't get to watch him grow up. But she is reading books on people who have beaten really dreadful prognoses. She says their cancers make hers look like poison oak.

I'm just trying to stay faithful. I heard this amazing East

Indian doctor talking about autistic kids back East who were so severely withdrawn that if you stood them up, they'd just fall over. They'd make no effort to stand or even to shield their faces when they fell. Then these people working with them discovered that if they ran a rope from one end of the room to the other and stood the kids up so that they were holding on to the rope, the kids would walk across the room. So over the months they kept putting up thinner and thinner pieces of rope, until they were using something practically invisible, like fishing line, and the kids would *still* walk across the room if they could hold on to it. And then—and this really seems like a brainstorm—the adults cut the fishing line into pieces, into twelve-inch lengths or something, and handed one to each kid. The kids would still walk. What an amazing statement of faith. I told this to Pammy, but she didn't really respond right away. She went over to where Sam was playing and sat down next to him and said, "Mommy's a religious fanatic." She held him in her lap while he played with his toys, and she made him laugh, and then she started to cry.

"We need to get some," she said sometime later.

"Some what?" I asked.

"Some fishing line."

I haven't been to the store yet, but I feel like every time the phone rings and it's Pammy and she needs to talk about this horrible thing that's happening now, or, come to think of it, every night when I don't get any sleep and then the baby is crying to be fed at 6:00 A.M., or every day when I sit down and try to get a little bit of writing done, that I am clutching my little piece of fishing line as I go to the phone or the crib or my desk.

MAY 3

She calls me in the mornings to check in, and we go over her stuff, any new information or thoughts she might have, and then she always says to please, please tell her every single new thing Sam is doing.

He pulls himself up on the little fence we erected around the floor heater to keep him from crawling on it. It is very secure, screwed into the wall. But he shakes it for ten minutes at a time like he's trying to tear it down, like there's not a jail in the land that can hold him. All he wants to do is to stand up; he falls down a lot, bumps his head, cries, and then wants to get right back up.

He thinks I'm hilarious. We have a game where I ever so slowly scan the ceiling, like I'm watching for enemy planes, and he watches intently, getting increasingly more anxious as I lower my gaze, and then when I suddenly look right at him, he screams with joy and surprise like I just doused him with water. Then I do it again, slowly scanning the ceiling, and he gets very somber, and turns his eyes upward, and his mouth opens a little. . . .

He also likes to put the cat's little toy ball in his mouth. It's slightly bigger than a Ping-Pong ball, and I know it's too big for him to swallow. It pulls his top lip and his lower jaw so far down that he looks exactly like a little transvestite Eleanor Roosevelt. I can't take my eyes off him. And then I remember Pammy and am hit with terror. My mind whirs with awful fantasies of the future, a rehashing of what happened to Dad. I do everything possible to find my faith and to get back into the now. I try to tell myself really gently, Okay, okay, enough mind-fucking already—now back to our regularly scheduled broadcast.

MAY 4

Pammy, Sam, and I went to Marine World today. Pammy starts chemo tomorrow, and this just seemed the right thing to do. We had a ball. The best part is the dolphin and killer whale show; the two killer whales are unspeakably beautiful. Sam was blown away at the sight of them, just delirious, but then again he's blown away by the kitty.

The three dolphins who open the show kept coming out before their cue, and their trainer kept sending them back and seemed genuinely annoyed. He explained to us that they were relatively new and that it would take a while for them to get it exactly right, and then they would come racing out again without having been summoned. They were sent back out of our sight (it was actually sort of tense), and Pammy whispered to me, "I'm afraid we're going to hear three shots ring out any minute. . . ."

Pammy and I are both very scared and angry, but her spirits are fantastic. All sorts of people have given her copies of a tape by this healer named Louise Hay, who is very popular in the AIDS community. Hay's position is that unresolved stuff from our past causes us to get—to give ourselves—cancer and that self-love will heal us, that it is our responsibility to cure ourselves. Every morning you stand in front of the mirror and say, "I *love* you." Well, needless to say, it makes Pammy see red. It makes her see every color of the rainbow. It just makes her nuts. So every time I mention anyone who doesn't seem to be doing well—like this guy we know who keeps getting these headaches—Pammy will say nonchalantly, "I think it's brain tumors. I'd better go ahead and send him one of my Louise Hay tapes."

It's almost impossible to change Sam these days. You'd think I was trying to brand him.

M A Y   6

Mom and Aunt Pat baby-sat Sam today so Pammy and I could go to a matinee. Pammy didn't buy any chocolate, just popcorn and a mineral water, and she kept trying to make me give her another handful of M&Ms.

"Why didn't you buy your own?" I whispered.

"I didn't know I wanted them so much. Will you go buy me some?"

"No," I said. "I'm trying to watch the movie." There was a silence.

"I have *cancer*," she said. So I clapped my hand over my eyes in the most exasperated way and poured a bunch of candy into her outstretched palm.

A few minutes later I felt her tugging on my sleeve. I looked over with great hostility. *"Now what?"*

"Can I have one more handful?" she asked. Every few minutes I'd feel her tug on my sleeve again, and I'd turn to find her holding out her palm, beaming at me, and if I shook my head she'd whisper terrible things to me about her cancer, about how weak she felt, until finally I ran out of M&Ms. Then she tried to get me to go buy us another box, and I told her she was in danger of becoming a parasite. She laughed for so long that people in front of us turned and glared.

M AY 8

Pammy and I went next door to
pay a visit on my neighbors this afternoon and got involved
in a rather unpleasant ethical consultation. I'd never actually
met them before. I am not much of a mingler. Both the
husband and wife are strange, dour characters, and someone
must have recently given them massive wind chimes, because
I noticed them ringing last night when I was trying to sleep.
By about 2:00 A.M., I felt I might have a complete nervous
breakdown if they didn't stop chiming, but then the wind died
down. Halfway through my work this morning, as I was
hurrying to get a book review written, the wind picked back
up and the chiming began again. I know they are supposed to
be very lovely and spiritual and soothing, but this is only the
case when they are yours. Trying to work with them chiming
away was like having Jimi Hendrix jamming over there on top
of the roof. I felt very meek and apologetic and cringey about
the whole thing, but I simply could not stand them. Luckily,
Pammy came over in a bad mood, loaded for bear, angry and
scared about everything and a little sick from the chemo. So
we stormed over, and I let her do most of the talking. She was
very adamant and kept mentioning that I am a writer and I
need for things to be very quiet so that I can hear my characters speak. I felt like when you're little and your parents are

standing there talking sternly to someone who has hurt or betrayed you and you just want to climb into the backseat of the car and lie down on the floor with your car coat pulled over you. Needless to say, the neighbors were not happy about our request. They were actually appalled, like I had asked them not to wear shoes around the house because their footsteps were too loud. But they did take down the chimes. Now it is very peaceful again here under the redwoods.

I remember going to a party at Pammy's house when I was six years old. I've known her since before Jesus left Chicago, and I don't remember her ever even getting the flu.

MAY 9

Having a baby is a terrible drain on the resources. I had no idea. I'm not suggesting that he's a deadbeat, but I must say he's not bringing in any money on his own. Lately he sits around in his underwear all day playing the harmonica, which is great, I approve of his choice of instruments. I mean, I don't want him to turn out to be Donovan. I want him to be able to play the *blues*. But still, it's so expensive and time-consuming to have a baby, you might as well keep hothouse orchids. At least you can sell them.

Today I've felt all day like we are the Joads. Everything we own is so cruddy-looking and secondhand. Even the cat is secondhand. My brother Steve and I found her wrapped in a plastic garbage bag by the side of the road on Christmas Eve three years ago. Someone had just chucked her out the window of a car. We heard a kitty crying and then walked past a Hefty bag sealed with rubber bands from which the sound was clearly emanating. "I don't hear anything," I said at first, putting my fingers in my ears. I did not want a cat, did not in fact want any dependents. I had been sober six months, and it was all I could do to take care of myself. "You don't hear the cat crying in that Hefty bag?" my brother asked. I shook my head and then sighed. But she's a great cat.

All the other babies have beautiful little nurseries, and Sam just has the corner of my horrible hovel of a room. There are three feet of floor space between his crib and the platform where my mattress is, and that's it. There's a broken-down dresser with a thin foam pad on it that we use for the changing table. It's too hideous for words. It's Tobacco Road.

> People who write novels
> Often live in hovels.

I'm sure someone else said that before me. I hate everything.

We sat and watched Bush on the news tonight, full of his usual bombastic suckitude. Sam was cheering him on and I was crying out, "No, no, darling, this is the enemy," but Sam was totally wild in his enthusiasm and support, like we were watching the Lakers beat the Celtics. A mother worries.

My plans for molding him into the leader of the rebel forces do not seem to be going very well. I think of all those pacifists in the sixties and seventies whose children chewed their toast into the shape of guns. Sam will be one of those children. I can see it all now. He will probably be a Young Republican by the age of eight and want to spend his summers at camp with other little conservative boys and girls, singing patriotic songs in shorts and knee-high socks, holding his briefcase in his lap. He'll pound the table jovially and cry out, "We're table one and we want the salt!" and then help plot the forced internment of the left wing in America. Then he'll come home from camp, and everywhere I go in our house, his eyes will seem to follow me, and when I notice this, he will give me thin smiles.

MAY 10

Pammy got through her first round of chemo fine. We had a wonderful talk about it late last night. She said she's just going to do what her doctor says—no New Age crystal Cosmica Rama stuff, no dietary changes. She said that if one more person tells her that she probably shouldn't have wine at night and that she should be eating a lot of broccoli, she is going to stick a pencil through her throat. "I am not going to eat broccoli," she said. "I'm sorry, I'm just not. When they get their tumors, *they* can eat broccoli. I will go to their houses and steam it for them, but I will not be eating it." She's tiptoeing into the very beginning of some sort of relationship with God, or with a higher power, or something, but it is very hard for her to believe. "Look," she said, "if you had parents like mine, if you grew up in a family as secretive and pathetic as mine, I don't think you'd believe either."

I said, "We *all* grew up in that family. I mean, this is America, honey." I recommended that she think of all the women who have most adored her in her life and to come up with a sense of God based on that kind of love, on the sense of protectedness that it gives you to be loved by a really fine woman, a sense of some mysterious regenerative force at the center of things that is maybe just love. She said with great surprise, "I didn't know you could *do* that," and I said, "Oh, yeah, you can do anything you want," and by this morning she'd found a picture of a big cat licking a little cat. She's a great cat lover, and it stuck. So at the hospital this morning, as she sat in the doctor's office getting the chemo IV, and then as she sat around at home all day waiting to become Linda Blair, she said she'd picture this big cat licking her gently and carrying her in its mouth to safer places.

Well, the Joads had an okay day today, although now Sam screams loudly when he's frustrated, like if he can't open a certain drawer. I guess he's developing will. I don't think I like this in a baby. We drove up to see my therapist today, and I was listening to this sort of goopy Christian music on the radio, trying to check out because I'm just not feeling great these days. My stomach aches with anxiety about Pammy, and my self-esteem is about one notch lower than Kafka's cockroach. We're broke, and I'm fat and lonely. All of a sudden I tuned in to Sam, who was not paying any attention to me, chattering away in Serbo-Croatian, and I could hear suddenly that the song of life was playing and that Sam was singing it. So I turned off the radio and listened to Sam and got the spiritual hit I was starving for.

He sounded like a bevy of drunken doves.

MAY 12

He continues to love the kitty more than life itself. He crawls or rushes over to her in his walker and then pulls at her face and ears passionately, while screaming in almost anguished love, like a Beatles fan at Candlestick Park.

I'm very lonely. Neshama was talking today about her marriage with John, who is kind of a loner, very bright and eccentric. They're both in their fifties, married twenty-five years, and she said, "We're Rilke's 'Solitudes' in motion. Maybe less and less in motion. . . ." That's what I want so much.

Pammy came by with strawberry sorbet and the new *People* magazine. I felt like God had reached down and touched me. She's so incredibly kind to us. It would be much easier to think of losing her if she weren't so goddamn kind. Maybe I will talk to her about this tomorrow.

I remember how much her crazy drunken mother used to smoke when we were young, and I wonder if that has anything to do with Pammy's cancer. Her mother would blow smoke into your face, even when you were a little kid. She had this elaborate inhaling technique—I think it was French—where she'd take a hit and it would pour out over her top lip like a reverse waterfall. It was really quite beautiful. And then she'd blow it into our faces.

Somehow, somewhere along the line, Pammy forgave her parents. I heard someone say once that forgiveness is having given up all hope of having had a better past. And this is why Pammy is so powerful.

MAY 16

Sam is recovering from a burn on his hand that he got at my friend Alice's on Sunday night. Alice had been cooking a roast all afternoon and opened the oven door to take it out. Sam was in his walker, and in a flash, like a speed skater, he darted over and put his palms down flat on the opened door. Our friend Dennis rushed him to the sink and put his hands under cold water for the longest time, but there were blisters. Still, Sam seemed okay. He was sort of unattached to the pain. I was reminded of the time the kitty jumped onto a spike near the houseboat where we lived and had a huge hole in her chest, so big you could see her lungs, and how, after getting it stitched up, she was completely done with it.

Now, me, if I'd had burnt palms, I'd milk them for all they

were worth. I'd go about for weeks holding out my little paws as though they had been run over by a truck.

Megan puts some New Age hippie aloe juice on Sam's burns every day, but she really only does it for herself. I, the old addict, keep thinking he needs some heavy pharmaceuticals, when actually he seems to be just fine.

Pammy came by today and feels so nauseated from the chemo that she can't even drink tea anymore, only water. And it has to be room temperature. She said she wants me to help her write a chemo cookbook, that we could make a fortune off it, and I said, What would be in it? And she said, Smoothies, toast, and room temperature tap water. That's all.

MAY 18

Sam and I sat out on the steps last night for a long time, and he fell asleep in my arms. It's so easy to have religious awe when you're outside at night. It's even easier when you're in the mountains, especially during a thunderstorm. Boy, do you feel like an aphid, and boy, are you glad there are other aphids around.

MAY 20

Pammy had her first, and maybe last, THC experience last night. Pot is supposed to help chemo-related nausea. I remember my dad using it a number of times during his chemo and not liking it at all, because it made him so aware of every single thing he was feeling, and he was feeling so bad. But yesterday Pammy took a capsule of Marinol, pharmaceutical marijuana, even though she hates being stoned. I called her around 5:00 because I was feeling sort of lost and sad, and she told me she had taken the Marinol and was just waiting for her husband to come home, somewhat high but really glad to listen. So I talked for a while, poured out all my sorrows and this quiet philosophical stream of consciousness, and she listened attentively and every so often at just the right moment said, "Mm-hmm." It made me feel all choked up with wonder and gratitude for the intimacy and tenderness of our relationship. Then I'd say something that was a thinly veiled plea for some advice or a pep talk, and she'd just say, "Hmmmm," like she knew I was going to be able to answer my own question in a moment. It seemed such a spiritually enlightened position to take. This went on for quite some time. It was so comforting. She was so present and so supportive, in a nonverbal way, and then I apologized for going on so long and said, "God, you're such an incredible listener, Pammy. Were you able to follow all that?" and she didn't answer for a moment. Then she said dreamily, "No, not really; I was just sort of vegging out on your voice tones."

Sam can climb stairs now. I don't think this is good news.

Today at church he played with the kids in the back room for the first time. He was in his walker, and these little kids are possibly the most stunningly gorgeous people on earth. They adore him, and they push him hard in his walker from one person to the next, all the way across the room—it's like a cross between curling and dwarf-tossing. All the little kids including Sam roar with laughter, like they're all in love.

MAY 31

Sam was nine months old the other day. Steve brought him his first gun, all nicely wrapped up, but it turned out that he had just borrowed it from a friend's kid in order to get a rise out of me. Steve is hypervigilant about not being made into a father figure. Every so often he calls me on this, on my secretly wishing he could be Sam's surrogate father. I always lie at first and insinuate that this is all in his mind, but then I go into another room and all but snap my fingers, like "Rats! Foiled again." Finally I end up confessing to Steve that maybe I do try to manipulate things along these lines, and I always end up crying because it makes me feel so vulnerable to be so pathetic and transparent. Steve pats me a lot, tenderly, and then he gives the baby a bath or in some other way pours on the avuncular love.

I don't remember who said this, but there really are places in the heart you don't even know exist until you love a child. Sam's been teaching me how to play again, at my ripe old age. His favorite thing right now is for me to hide a Cheerio in my mouth and then to let it peek out a tiny bit, and he goes in after it with this great frantic concentration, like it's a diamond.

JUNE 5

We're sick, for the second time in two weeks. I can't believe it. I never used to get sick. These babies are all carriers. And then Pammy, who was all better from the cold she caught from us last week, came by with groceries, determined not to pick Sam up, just to drop off some supplies. But it was impossible for her not to hold him for a second, and of course he slimed her a few times, sucking on her nose. So she's sick again, too, and needs more antibiotics. I feel completely responsible. But she said it was good that we figured out in her first month of chemo instead of, say, her fifth that we have to be *extremely* careful and to err on the side of caution. She also said that she liked sitting around with an illness with which she was familiar. It was like wearing an old worn, soft shirt, just to have a sore throat and head cold. She said she was sitting around almost savoring it, sitting in the rocking chair a lot, holding her imaginary piece of fishing line.

June 14

We're doing more or less okay. There are days when it feels like *The Seventh Seal* with diaper rash and milky bras, but right now we're sort of lurching along. I am having to spend so much time trying to keep the faith. Otherwise I spin off into tremendous anxiety.

Sam is growing so fast that it almost makes me light-headed. It's time-lapse photography speeded up. Maybe I shouldn't feed him so much. I feel like he's not even a baby anymore. He's becoming a young adult.

They get so smart so fast. For instance, there's been another new development that I'm not sure I like. He seems to have picked up a memory somewhere. In the old days—in his youth—you could hide something you didn't want him to have behind your back and that would be the end of it. He'd maybe look around for a split second with this benevolent look on his face, like "Well, for Chrissakes, that's funny, it's gone; oh, well, now I can't even remember what it is that's gone, but who cares." Now he looks at me blankly when I first take something away, and then he lunges at me, like he'll kick my teeth in to get it back.

He has a frantic craving to be vertical. Every second he pulls himself up to a standing position again. You'd think he'd just spent six months in a body cast. He is so full of energy and muscle, teething, ranting, crazed, but he's the best baby you could ever hope for. Still a baby, though, which is to say, still periodically a pain in the neck. Donna was saying the other day that she knows this two-year-old who's really very together and wonderful a lot of the time, really the world's best two-year-old, but then she added, "Of course, that's like saying Albert Speer was the nicest Nazi. He was still a Nazi."

When Sam's having a hard time and being a total baby about the whole thing, I feel so much frustration and rage and self-doubt and worry that it's like a mini-breakdown. I feel like my mind becomes a lake full of ugly fish and big clumps of algae and coral, of feelings and unhappy memories and re-hearsals for future difficulties and failures. I paddle around in it like some crazy old dog, and then I remember that there's a float in the middle of the lake and I can swim out to it and lie down in the sun. That float is about being loved, by my friends and by God and even sort of by me. And so I lie there and get warm and dry off, and I guess I get bored or else it is human nature because after a while I jump back into the lake, into all that crap. I guess the solution is just to keep trying to get back to the float.

This morning Sam woke at 4:00, so I put him in bed with me, nursed him for a long time, and then fell back asleep in the dark with him nestled up against me. The only light came from this dimmer switch on the wall by my side of the bed. There is a foot of carpeted space between my mattress and the wall, and the dimmer switch is on the wall about two feet off the floor. It is lit so you can find it in the dark, but it's underneath a beautiful piece of cloth I've hung there, white with the prettiest parrots on it, so the dimmer glows golden beneath the cloth like Tinkerbell's light. Anyway, I kept hear-ing Sam scooting around next to me in the dark, and I kept saying, "Shh, shh, go back to sleep," half-dozing. Then it became totally silent and I almost fell asleep, but I opened my eyes a crack and looked up to see Sam standing between the bed and the wall, with one hand on either side of the dimmer, his face a few inches away from it so that he was lit by its light. He looked like he was in joyful supplication, or an ecstatic trance, like the little boy in *Close Encounters.*

JUNE 16

This memory thing is really interesting. Before, every time Sam went into a room—the bathroom, for instance—he would be almost beside himself with wonder and amazement, like it was his first trip to FAO Schwarz. Now he recognizes it. It's not quite old-hat yet, but he sees the bathtub and he remembers that he loves it and he tries to thrust and squirm his way over to it. It's funny that he loves the bathtub so much. He didn't always. But mostly he loves to toss stuff into the tub when it's empty, and then he loves to gaze endlessly down into it, with wonder, like it's a garden in full bloom.

He's heavily into flinging things. He dismantles everything he can get his hands on, pulling every possible book and chotchke off every possible table and shelf and flinging them over his shoulder. It's like living with a Hun, or Sunny Barger, the old leader of the Hell's Angels. You can almost hear

"RIDE HARD!" ringing through the chambers of his mind: "RIDE HARD! DIE FREE!"

It's gratuitous looting. He almost never actually *takes* anything and crawls away with it, but he'll get to the coffee table and systematically, often without any expression, lift and then drop or fling every single magazine, book, cup, or whatever to the ground. His grim expression suggests he's got a lot to do and just really doesn't want to be bothered until he's done.

Pammy is pretty sick from the chemo. It's so bizarre to write those words. It's like saying, "Sam is having trouble with the metal plate in his head." It's something that simply can't be happening. So it isn't quite so scary and painful as it might be, since it doesn't feel like it's really happening a lot of the time. It makes me feel totally in the dark and about eight years old. I'm trying to keep my faith high, but I feel sort of disgusted and puzzled by God right now. It makes me think of Sam's gratuitous looting; God standing there bored at his table, dropping, or letting people's lives drop, to the floor. It's like he doesn't even care, isn't even paying attention. It's like James Joyce said: he's doing his nails.

I have a friend named Anne, this woman I've known my entire life, who took her two-year-old up to Tahoe during the summer. They were staying in a rented condominium by the lake. And of course, it's such a hotbed of gambling that all the rooms are equipped with these curtains and shades that block out every speck of light so you can stay up all night in the casinos and then sleep all morning. One afternoon she put the baby to bed in his playpen in one of these rooms, in the pitch-dark, and went to do some work. A few minutes later she heard her baby knocking on the door from inside the room, and she got up, knowing he'd crawled out of his playpen. She went to put him down again, but when she got to the door, she found he'd locked it. He had somehow managed to push in the little button on the doorknob. So he was calling to her, "Mommy, Mommy," and she was saying to him, "Jiggle the doorknob, darling," and of course he didn't speak much English—mostly he seemed to speak Urdu. After a moment, it became clear to him that his mother *couldn't* open the door, and the panic set in. He began sobbing. So my friend ran around like crazy trying everything possible, like trying to get the front door key to work, calling the rental agency where she left a message on the machine, calling the manager of the condominium where she left another message, and running back to check in with her son every minute or so. And there he was in the dark, this terrified little child. Finally she did the only thing she could, which was to slide her fingers underneath the door, where there was a one-inch space. She kept telling him over and over to bend down and find her fingers. Finally somehow he did. So they stayed like that for a really long time, on the floor, him holding onto her fingers in the dark. He stopped

220

crying. She kept wanting to go call the fire department or something, but she felt that contact was the most important thing. She started saying, "Why don't you lie down, darling, and take a little nap on the floor?" and he was obviously like "Yeah, *right*, Mom, that's a great idea, I'm feeling so nice and relaxed." So she kept saying, "Open the door now," and every so often he'd jiggle the knob, and eventually, after maybe half an hour, it popped open.

I keep thinking of that story, how much it feels like I'm the two-year-old in the dark and God is the mother and I don't speak the language. She could break down the door if that struck her as being the best way, and ride off with me on her charger. But instead, via my friends and my church and my shabby faith, I can just hold onto her fingers underneath the door. It isn't enough, and it is.

JUNE 18

Peg came over with dinner tonight and told me about this dumb schmaltzy poem she heard someone read at an AA meeting. It got me thinking. It was about how while we are on earth, our limitations are such that we can only see the underside of the tapestry that God is weaving. God sees the topside, the whole evolving portrait and its amazing beauty, and uses us as the pieces of thread to weave the picture. We see the glorious colors and shadings, but we also see the knots and the threads hanging down, the thick lumpy patches, the tangles. But God and the people in heaven with him see how beautiful the portraits in the tapestry are. The poem says in this flowery way that faith is about the willingness to be used by God wherever and however he most needs you, most needs the piece of thread that is your life. You give him your life to put through his needle, to use as he sees fit. I hope Sam's is a very long piece of thread. Please God let it be longer than mine.

Pammy's looks like it's going to be too short. I wanted it to be longer than mine, too. But maybe hers is being used to do an exquisite bit of detailing—a tiny furled bud, requiring lots and lots of quick little stitches because you can't convey the bud without all that convolution, can't show how much life there is inside: a tiny leaf, the blossom.

JUNE 20

I swear Sam is a week away from walking. He crawls everywhere and climbs everything. Yesterday I was in the bathroom, and Megan was with him in the kitchen, letting him crawl around. She went to the front door to let the kitty out, and when she got back, Sam had climbed the four steps of the ladder to the loft and, as Megan reports, was sitting on the mattress like the Buddha, very pleased with himself in the most casual possible way, like "Hey, baby, just hanging out here on my mom's bed. Come on up and have a beer!"

Tonight at Rex and Dudu's when I came to pick him up, he was playing catch with them, pushing a tennis ball across the coffee table to them, catching it when they would push it back, concentrating as hard as Nolan Ryan pitching another no-hitter.

Earlier today he pulled a TV dinner table down on himself when I was doing something in the kitchen. He fell down on the carpet and lay there with this two-pound table on top of him, wild-eyed with the drama of it all, like he was Joe Ben in *Sometimes a Great Notion* who gets pinned under the log. He looked up at me, not crying but tortured, like "You ignorant incompetent slut—*you* did this to me; you're supposed to be watching me, but nooooooo . . ."

June 21

This boy can dance, Mama; he still can't walk, but he pulls himself into a standing position, holds on to the couch or chair or leg or whatever is nearby, and begins to bounce and gyrate. This boy can rock and roll. It's such a miracle. It seems that only yesterday he was so pupal, and now he's Michael Jackson.

The guy who loves George Bush and doesn't give head called yesterday and also today. There's a part of me that wants to go ahead and give him a whirl because he's so smart and funny. But I know that he's got a mean streak, that his girlfriends all end up feeling ripped off and shut out. Then when they break up with him, he loses his mind completely and throws himself at them and says all the right things and takes them for the romantic weekend sail on the delta. As my agent once said of another man, he has the soul of a trapped rat. The girlfriends always end up going back for a few more rounds, and the exact same pattern plays out. Who needs it? Peggy once gave me the best definition of insanity, something they apparently say in AA, that insanity is doing the same thing over and over, each time expecting a different result. So I'm trying to resist—he asked me out on an actual date today and I made up an excuse—but I find myself craving the excitement, the danger.

224

My life has become so mundane. The biggest thrill left for me, the only time I really feel I'm courting danger, is when I'm washing my hair and I step directly under the shower spray and let the water begin to stream down my forehead, but I wait a split second to close my eyes so that the shampoo gets dangerously close to blinding me. Whoa! What a rush!

I got out the Polaroid I took when I was pregnant, of the photographs of me pregnant and at seven years old and the sonogram photo of Sam, all under the arms of the cross, and I can still get that sense that we are a complete family unit, but sometimes I'm so hungry for a partner, a lover. One thing I know for sure, though, is that when you are hungry, it is an act of wisdom each time you turn down a spoonful if you know that the food is poisoned.

JUNE 22

Sam got a tooth. I saw a little flash of white in his mouth way over to the right and didn't think much of it because I was expecting his first teeth to be either the two top front ones or two bottom front ones. This one is way over to the east. I decided the whiteness was a sore, baby herpes or something even worse, because I couldn't feel a sharp little point, but Pammy insisted it was a tooth. Then the two of us took him in to see the doctor for his regular checkup, and I mentioned it. I said he seemed to have a sore in his mouth. Pammy said it was a tooth, and Dr. James felt it for a nanosecond, looked up at Pammy, and they smiled conspiratorially at each other. Then they both looked at me and shook their heads. I'm so glad I didn't share with James what I actually thought, which was that it was infant melanoma.

The drool is immense. There are rivers of drool all day now, almost biblical, like the waters of Babylon. He has a drool rash on his chin. It made me think of his old baby-acne days when Steve used to call him Pizza Face. A friend of ours watched him drooling away like a Saint Bernard puppy and finally said to him, "Hey, kid? Get a lip."

I hope he gets his daddy's teeth. Actually I have no idea what his daddy's teeth look like, since he had almost all crowns, the result of a bad car accident a few years ago. For all I know, before the accident he used to look like an alligator gar or a moray eel. I also don't know if his original teeth were strong or not, but they've got to be better than mine. Mine are like chalk. Little bits are breaking off all the time, and I've had more cavities in my life than anyone I know. I have so many crowns that I actually can't fit them all in my mouth—I have to keep a bunch of them in the drawer by my bedside table. Of course, Sam's growing up with fluoridated water. I taught a writing course at UC Davis one semester, and one afternoon we had some time to kill, so I asked my students to take out a piece of paper and write about some really horrible humiliating frightening thing they have to do periodically, like going to the dentist. They all looked at me like I had just started taking off my clothes, because it turned out that a good two-thirds of them had never even *had* a cavity. I mean, it was awful, and then they were all sort of laughing at me as I stood there with bits of my teeth breaking off, and pretty soon they all looked like hallucinated troglodyte versions of Mary Tyler Moore.

JUNE 25

It seems cavalier to go out and have fun when Pammy is home with her husband being so sick from the chemo, but for one thing I need to make a living. I ended up going out with the gang to do a food review the other night. I was feeling very low, in quicksand, and like I wasn't well enough to be out in public trying to be interesting. All I wanted to do was to stay home and sit on the couch necking with my fear and depression. But I made myself show up, and it got me unstuck. Like they say, take the action and the insight will follow. There's still real life going on out there, and it was such a nice break to take my extension cord and plug into it for a while.

Bill was all edgy because the restaurant we went to smelled so strongly of garlic and he's badly allergic to it, so as usual we tried to order as many dishes as possible without it. We always order family-style. But I was whining about wanting to try this roast Dungeness crab with billions of cloves of garlic. I said in this conciliatory way to Bill, "Look, honey, if you'll just let us order this one thing, you can order something fabulous that *I* can't eat," and he looked at me bitterly and said, "And what would that be, Annie? Thorns?" I laughed so hard that it broke up the thin candy shell of fear that was covering my heart, and I could breathe again. I think that's what they mean by grace—the divine assistance for regeneration.

JUNE 27

Peg and Pammy both came over for lunch, and then we all took Sam for a walk in the park. He swung in the baby swing for over half an hour. His Big Brother Brian has been bringing him here since he was a few months old, putting him in these swings ever since he could hold his neck up. We have come here a lot together, too, Sam and Pammy and I, especially in the last couple of months. Sam is our anchor. Without him as our counterbalance to Pammy's cancer, we would float off into outer space on fear. It crossed my mind recently that maybe we were using him like a drug, to avoid the terrible feelings we are having. But drugs take you away from what is in front of you, whereas Sam *is* what's in front of us. He's not the drug, he's the reality. I think this is why Pammy asks every day for the specific details of what he's up to.

When we first brought him to this park, he was an aging infant. In one of the swings, he looked like a fragile little egg with the face of Tweety Bird, swinging back and forth with a slightly perplexed expression. Then he went through a stage where Pammy said he looked just like one of those Al Capp characters called shmoos. Now he is cool and intense, like the child of James Dean and one of those aliens you see in the tabloids who resemble giant babies with saucer eyes. He is going to follow in my footsteps as a swing junkie, though. Anyone looking at me as a child on swings should have known that I would grow up to be an addict. Swings were one of my favorite things about life. When it was your turn, you'd sit on the piece of wood or the tire or the knot at the bottom of the rope, and your friends would wind you up in one direction until you and the rope couldn't be twisted any tighter and then they'd let you go, and you'd unwind faster and faster, out of control until it felt like your head was going to spin off your neck. You'd just lose your mind joyously in the whirling wheel of green foliage you'd see every time you opened your eyes.

Everyone but me would eventually want to go home. Red-faced, exhausted, my nerves jumping, I'd be pleading to spin one more time, just one more time. Peg said today in the park that she was also this way—Peg who, like me, ended up snorting coke like a truffle pig. Along these lines (no pun intended), Sam's expressions were somewhat alarming today: he completely gets it, was totally into it. Everything in his face was saying, "Swing; *swing.*"

Peg pushed Sam while Pammy and I sat beside them in the swings for bigger kids. Peg had treated herself to a manicure the day before, and she told me that the manicurist had her soak her fingertips in a bowl of warm soapy water and *marbles,* of all things. "What were the marbles for?" I asked. "So that your fingers don't get bored," she replied. "So they have something friendly to do while they're soaking. It was lovely. They clicked softly between your fingers, and the water was like velvet." I've never had a manicure, but I could picture and hear it perfectly. It made me think of how Sam is in my mind when we are apart. In the old days, before Sam, my mind would be filled with fantasies and ambitious thoughts and terrible worry about every aspect of my life, including global starvation and the environment and nuclear power and weapons and friends dying, and now that all still goes on, but there are a lot of times in a very real sense when images of him give my mind something friendly to play with, something lovely for a change to click between its fingers.

The three of us women sat for long periods without talking, while Sam played in the sand. We would talk with great animation for a while and then be quiet again. My father and I could do this, too. It is so profoundly comforting and beautiful, the minuet of old friendships.

JUNE 29

Every so often Sam will be standing up, holding on to something, like the coffee table, for instance, and he will have finished his work there—that is, he will have already flung everything to the floor—and all of a sudden he'll let go with both hands and stand there for a few seconds. It's totally charged time, like the moments right before lightning. Then you can see concern cross his face, and on the inside he's going, "Yo! Holy *shit!*" When he starts to wobble, he reaches for the table again to steady himself.

JUNE 30

I do my food review every month for *California*, and my book review for *Mademoiselle*, and a pretty flabby job of trying to keep this journal up to date. I take notes and dick around with possible scenes for a novel, but I don't feel like writing much else. Certainly not a long sustained piece of fiction. I can't really remember how you do it. But I just remembered the other day a weekend I spent with my family at our cabin in Bolinas when I was seven or eight and my older brother was nine or ten. He had this huge report on birds due in school and hadn't even started it, but he had tons of bird books around and binder paper and everything. He was just too overwhelmed, though. And I remember my dad sitting down with him at the dining table and putting his hands sternly on my brother's shoulders and saying quietly, patiently, "Bird by bird, buddy; just take it bird by bird." That is maybe the best writing advice I have ever heard.

July I

I just got off the phone with Pammy. It is almost 11:00 at night. As usual she wanted to hear every detail of our day, even though it was so late and she was tired. She's so nauseated that it's like a sweet form of chemo—a benevolent drug—for her to hear about Sam, in the flush and fullness of his babyhood, growing up. I had so much to tell her tonight, Sam had such a busy day, and Pammy understands as well as anyone alive what a miracle it is that life keeps making itself anew and flourishing and that we can all tap into it.

He had his first informal communion today, his first cheeseburger, and his first black eye. To begin backwards, tonight at the Smiths he had climbed up the wooden steps that go from their kitchen to the bedrooms. He and Big Sam were playing at the top of them, and all of a sudden he tumbled and fell all the way down, bouncing like a rubber baby. All of us were moving in slow motion, like we were underwater, to catch him, but couldn't, and he ended up at the bottom of the stairs having hit his eye on a corner. He cried, I cried, Big Sam cried. I absolutely knew in those first few seconds that he had a spinal cord injury and that his head was going to swell up with fluids like a medicine ball. It turned out that he was just fine. He was a little shaken up for a few minutes, and he started to get a shiner right away, but then of course he was ready to bolt right back up the stairs.

After church we stopped for lunch at a hamburger joint and split a cheeseburger. I tore his half into little pieces, and he ate almost the whole thing. There were some grilled onions stuck to his pieces, and mustard, and he ended up with this meaty, oniony, primordial manly breath. It was startling, like cigarettes on a nun's breath.

Earlier, during the service at church, when the bread and the tiny glasses of grape juice were passed to me, I gave Sam a bit of both. "Honey," I whispered to him, "this is the bread of heaven, and this is the blood," and he gobbled them both down and then burped, all but patting his big beer belly afterward.

JULY 7

It's been a hard day to get through, and we wouldn't have made it without Megan. She actually ministers to us, cooking me little treats, arranging for Sam to hand me a small bouquet of wildflowers when they come in from their walk. I was depressed all day, though. The good thing is that I have been sober four years today. I told

Sam this while he was nursing tonight and described what it used to be like. He hung on my every word. I have such a terribly checkered past. I am certainly not Donna Reed. I shouldn't even be alive. It's a small miracle. I sang him a talking-blues version of the Beatles' song "The Long and Winding Road." I sang to him about the long and winding road that had led to his door. I opened it and there he was, looking at me with those huge brown headlights of his.

Pammy is tired but otherwise doing okay with the chemo. She is so calm and spirited and optimistic, and I am such a mess. She told me a story a long time ago of being in Paris with her husband, driving around and around the Left Bank trying to hook up with a new friend, but she and her husband kept getting completely turned around. They were hot and frustrated and hopeless. So finally Pammy got out of the car and went into a café. She was so burnt she couldn't even try to speak French, so in English she said to the maître d', "We're lost," and he said in barely understandable English, "You are not lost; you are *right here.*" I try to remind myself of that every few days.

Sam has this one pose Pammy just adores, where he gets up on one knee and balances there, thoughtfully but with some confusion, like someone has just pulled a fast one and it is just beginning to dawn on him. She says it's very pre-Rodin: *The Sucker.*

She wants to get well so she and her husband can adopt. Sam has been her training baby. She hasn't cried very often since the diagnosis. I cry intermittently, like a summer rain. I don't feel racked by the crying; in fact, it hydrates me. Then rage wells up in me, and I want to take a crowbar to all the cars in the neighborhood.

Sam works so hard. He's so physical and alert and patient. His concentration is great, and he's got this fabulous sly and flirty look that renders you helpless, turns you to total mush. But sometimes he's also very willful. Other times he can't stop whining and clinging to me like some horrible horny Pekingese. It's hard. He's teething and uncomfortable and needy and looks like the inside of my soul when I first found out that Pammy was sick.

JULY 15

Whenever Sam does anything new or especially funny, my first thought is, Oh, Pammy will love this. Then she does. She does not laugh like a sick person, she laughs like she's always laughed. She came over this afternoon and almost immediately started to fall asleep on the couch. Sam stood holding himself up by her pant leg, waving goodnight to her. It may have been a coincidence. He can wave now, baby-style, hinging his fingers up and down over his palm. It's really more than either Pammy or I can handle. What next? I asked her. Juggling? Calligraphy?

He eats almost anything now. He took a nice fat ripe plum today and plowed into it like a gorilla, with buckets of juice and saliva pouring forth everywhere. Then he let the red skin emerge slowly from his mouth, like a rejected dollar bill from a change machine.

He has a slow, sexy smile. It just makes you crazy.

JULY 21

Pammy and her husband have gone away for a week, up the coast. Whenever we're apart, I'm afraid I will never see her again. She and her husband want to be by the ocean for a while, away from the phone, to sleep and just be together alone. Part of me thinks, How can she bear to be away from me, even for a day? A small bad part of me is glad to get a week off, too.

Sam is finally getting a second tooth. He's had that one huge snaggletooth way over on the side for so long. He's still not walking, but he holds onto couches and legs and dances to beat the band. He can entertain himself happily for twenty minutes at a stretch with coffee cans, paper bags, etc. I can see that he won't need me much longer.

His kissing has definitely changed. In the old days, up until last week, he'd graze you with his lips and flutter his eyelids on your face. Pammy always said he was gracing you. Now he gets a real lip lock on your cheek or mouth, like an eel. It's like kissing Elvis.

JULY 29

Pammy is back, and some of her strength is returning. There is color in her face again. We spent most of the day playing in her garden, watching Sam careen around, seemingly stoned on acid, gaping at butterflies and each dead leaf as if they were bejeweled.

He can growl now. Pammy kept growling at him, and he would growl back at her in this sexy, throaty way. It's not at all like a dog. Pammy compared it to Peter Boyle in _Young Frankenstein_, especially when he's in bed with Madeline Kahn at the end, lying there reading the _Wall Street Journal_. She lies beside him, saying in that amazing Madeline Kahn voice,

"Daddy this and Daddy that and I put two hampers in the bathroom, one for your regular clothes, and one for the poo-poo undies," and the Peter Boyle monster responds with these low throaty growls without looking up from his paper. Pammy was right: that's very close to what Sam sounds like.

I can't remember her ever having been so entirely happy. For twenty-five years now we have been so black-humored and cynical. There wasn't any of that today. It was so clean and bright, like all the dross had been scoured off. We sat on the grass in chaise longues, both of us in dark glasses and sun hats, Pammy growling at Sam, Sam growling back, me wiping my eyes. "Today I don't really care what happens," she said. "I'm just so glad to be here for this."

AUGUST 8

It's hard to keep up with this journal. It's all I can do to keep the two of us together and to get enough writing done to make a living and to keep the house from looking like something out of *God's Little Acre*. We're *totally* nouveau white trash. There are actually broken appliances out on the porch now.

I don't think I can climb up the steps here much longer.

There are about fifty of them, beautiful stone steps, but Sam is so big and heavy that trying to lug him and our groceries up them all the time is wearing me down. We need a bigger house on flatter ground.

My friend Ethan made me this wooden box about a foot high so I can do aerobic stepping—you get on and off it about two thousand times while listening to rock and roll, and you get sweaty and out of breath after about five minutes, but you make yourself do it for twenty. Everyone's doing it. It's the most now and happening form of exercise, although my personal belief is that thin smooth thighs do not necessarily speak of a rich inner life. So anyway, I had my step out on the porch with my broken appliances, and I was wearing a Walkman and listening to the Everly Brothers and sweating, when suddenly the Sears repair man appeared at the foot of the stairs. He was here to fix our upstairs neighbors' refrigerator, and as he trudged, panting, up the steep stone steps, he watched me get on and off my wooden step, and finally when he was close enough, he said, "I would not think you would need to do that, living here."

It was incredibly embarrassing.

AUGUST 9

Sam's *still* not walking, but he's finally getting lots of teeth all at once. When he bares his teeth at you in a smile, he looks a little like Martha Raye.

He's psychotically active, lovely, and social. Also, terribly willful. He makes a sharp cry when crossed, a string of sharp, vaguely Japanese sounds. Pammy calls it baby Tourette's.

He really loves music. Dudu and Rex are convinced he is a musical prodigy because he does his Michael Jackson dance routines to the operas they are always watching on PBS. I tell them that he is way behind schedule, that Mozart had already written symphonies by this age, but the three of them look at me with wounded defiance, like I am a cultural Philistine.

He does love music, though. He climbs in and out of the living room closet where I have a guitar on the floor, and he picks and strums it endlessly while babbling away. I call out requests to him—I say, "Hey, babe, do you know anything by Bob Dylan? Trini Lopez? Bobby Vee?" and sometimes he stops and appears to think about it for a minute. Then he'll launch into a heavy-metal version of "Lemon Tree," or sometimes "Jamaica Farewell."

. . .

In the morning, when he first wakes up and looks at me, it's with such joy and amazement that it's like someone had told him, before he went to sleep, that I had died.

AUGUST 10

Sam is learning to drink from a cup, but it is not going very well. Mostly he plunges his hand into glasses of water or juice, as if he has just had a sudden bout of Infant Hot Hand, as if steam will rise. He sloshes his hand around in the cup until the pain passes, and then every so often takes a tiny sip before plunging his hand back in. Then he hands the cup to you, and you are expected to take a sip, and it is clear by the look in his eyes that it will be a major emotional setback for him if you don't.

Sam and I took Pammy to the doctor in the afternoon. We are always expecting the doctor to say that mistakes were made and that Pammy is actually just fine, but what she said is that they are trying to control the cancer, that she doesn't think it can be cured per se, because it is too aggressive a strain and there were too many lymph nodes involved. Pammy didn't cry, and of course, in the car, I did. "Look," she said, "we've pretty much known that all along," and I hung my head and said, "I know," but when I got home I felt like I might go crazy with frustration. I cannot remember having such a huge rage inside me. I called Steve and cried, and he came up with a pizza for dinner. He did all these wonderful little errands around the house, fixing things, cleaning important windows. I felt like I could breathe again; I thought about how great it would be for Pammy—and how happy it would make me—if I went to her house and did the same sorts of things for her that Steve was doing for me. I ended up feeling just fine, against all odds. I thought, Boy, was that nutty old Mother Teresa right when she said that none of us can do great things, but that we can do small things with great love.

AUGUST I I

Last night was Peg's birthday, and Emmy and Bill had us to dinner. There was corn on the cob, which Sam loves because it's such a good teething product. So all of us were sitting around the table in the dining room eating dessert, having dumped all the chicken bones and corncobs into a garbage bag in the kitchen. Sam was scooting around the kitchen in his walker and got into the garbage and was playing with it, but Emmy said, "Let it go—whatever makes the little darling happy," because he'd been sort of fussy throughout dinner. The door of the dishwasher was open, and it turned out later that Sam had rather neatly stacked all the chicken bones and corncobs inside it. I said to Megan today, "He's so brilliant—he's trying to get the garbage clean," and she said, "Well, he *is* a Virgo."

Pammy and I still try on a daily basis to turn him against the Republicans. Pammy told him the other day while we were watching the news that Bush is a right-wing spider sack of lies and meanness, that he's the same kind of nightmare person as the dummy that comes to life in "The Twilight Zone." All that's missing, she said, is a little bit too much rouge on his cheeks and glycerin madness in his eyes. Then I told Sam that I fear Bush is secretly beginning to decompensate and one of these days will appear on the White House lawn covered with fingerpaints and breakfast foods, carrying an AK-47 and quoting from Mary Baker Eddy. They'll have to haul him off and pop him into the bin for a few years.

One thing that drives me crazy is when strangers ask, "How old is he?" and then, because they're stupid, go ahead and guess nine months, although he's very tall for his age. I tell them that he's almost a year old, and they can never admit that they were so far off, so they say, "Oh, he's small then, isn't he?" like he's a little peanut, like he's going to be Hervé Villechaize when he grows up, out on the lawn staring at the sky, crying, "Da plane, Boss, da plane!"

AUGUST 13

Today Sam and I went to the convalescent home, where my congregation conducts a worship service once a month. There was this new woman there, about eighty years old, and I went up to her wheelchair to say hi and to introduce her to Sam. The people at the home usually gape at Sam as if I've brought Jesus into the room with me. But this woman looked at him angrily and said, "Is that a *dog?*" And I said, "No, it's a baby." And she said meanly, "What *kind* of baby?" I tried to be Mother Teresa and to see Jesus in the distressing guise of the poor and incontinent, but I secretly wanted to push her wheelchair over and then kick her in the head.

AUGUST 20

Pammy's very sick from the latest round of chemo. My heart is broken.

I got a little bit interested in another man this week and sort of wanted to pursue it, to have someone to hold me and to be in love with, someone to do the big oompus-boompus with every few hours, but how can you go dancing under the fruit trees when someone like Pammy is so sick?

I feel sometimes that I let up and relaxed too much and that's why Pammy got sick. I got too tired and wasn't vigilant enough, so the flies got in through the window. This is infantile, but it keeps crossing my mind. It's like when Dylan Thomas came to America on an ancient propeller plane from London, and he said something like "I'm exhausted from trying to hold the plane up in the air."

I feel that the exhaustion and constant fear about Pammy make me like some little animal who lives on the ocean floor, who has an ink sack in its body, like a squid, that it's supposed to use for self-protection. But in my case, left to my own devices, I panic, and end up ink-jetting myself.

A u g u s t   2 4

Stop the presses. This just in: Sam walked last night at his Big Brother Brian and Diane's. They'd been taking care of him while I was at Cirque du Soleil, and they took him to a park for a picnic dinner. Diane pointed out a little girl who was smaller and younger than Sam but who was already walking and who had more teeth, and Diane said she really rubbed it in. An hour later, after I had arrived, Sam was leaning against the coffee table and let go, like he's done before, but then he walked three or four steps to me. We all went crazy. We just lost our minds. He looked mildly pleased. Then he did it a few more times. All the Smiths stopped by this morning, and he did it a few times again for them—four, five, six steps, looking absolutely wild in the eyes and triumphant the whole time.

By the afternoon he had forgotten how, and I went back to thinking that he would need leg braces and be one of Jerry's kids. At Rex and Dudu's tonight, though, he did it again, and again, and again. I can't really put my feelings about it into words. It's like breathing in cold clean mountain air and holding it for a little too long.

AUGUST 29

It's Sam's birthday today. He is one year old, my little walking dude. We had a little birthday dinner at Dudu and Rex's. Uncle Steve stopped by. There is a big party planned for the weekend at my Uncle Millard and Aunt Pat's. Absolutely everybody who is anybody will be there. I may hire the Blue Angels—the Air Force Precision Flyers—to buzz the house a couple of times.

He says "heeeee" for kitty—for our kitty and for all cats everywhere. He's very bright; he gets that from me. He can climb anything, and it is obvious that he is having huge testosterone surges. I still look at him and think, Where did you *come* from, little boy? How did you find your way?

I've been thinking about his birth all day, of walking to the drive-in with Pammy, of the male doctor at Kaiser who said the baby was flat. I remember walking down the corridor at Kaiser on the way out to Pammy's car, totally pissed off that there was not a room for me, and how really awful I felt and how much the contractions hurt. Pammy asked a nurse if I could get a Valium or something, and they looked at her like she was Jim Morrison. I thought about the ride over to Mount Zion in her car, which is this twenty-year-old Mercedes of her late mother's that we used to drive around in high school. I was bellowing "Fuuuuuuuuuck" at the top of my lungs. I kept remembering today the blood Pammy said looked like just a little crankcase oil down the back of my dress, of Carol, the angelic but no-nonsense resident who delivered Sam, and the nurses who'd read my books, and how deeply and quickly Pammy and Steve and I bonded with all of them. Pammy said later she felt like she'd even bonded with the equipment in that room; part of her wanted to take home the little stainless steel tray with the delivery intruments on it. I was remembering the magic of the epidural—the anesthesiologist's name was Merlin—and the long day on the monitor, with Pammy and Steve on either side of me, and then all the troubles. I can remember the feel of the sheets, warm from the dryer, on my body, and how hard I was shivering, and what despair I was feeling, and then Sam was born, purple as an eggplant, with his umbilical cord wrapped around his neck, but alive.

The mystery of this still leaves me scratching my head, that a baby was made in my body, grew on my milk, and lives here in the house with the kitty and me. It's too big to comprehend: Pammy said the other day that the thing happening in her body is so bizarre, so unthinkable, that trying to accept it is like being eight years old again with someone explaining to her that the light from the star she is staring at took twenty years to reach her. All she can do is to stand there staring at the star with a kind of fearful wonder, waiting for the information to make sense.

I pray all the time that we make it to the water, that the

birds don't pick Sam off. I'm afraid that they're going to get Pammy, though. I guess they get us all. When I held Sam alone for the first time, after Steve and Pammy had gone home the night that he was born, I was nursing him and feeling really spiritual, thinking, Please, please, God, help him be someone who feels compassion, who feels God's presence loose in the world, who doesn't give up on peace and justice and mercy for everyone. And then one second later I was begging, Okay, skip all that shit, forget it—just please, *please* let him outlive me.

He's in for it now, big-time, for all kinds of crazy shit. There are times when he experiences bad things, pain or fear or hurt feelings, and he clings to me like a wet cat, like a cat you're trying to bathe in the sink who tries to climb onto your head. It is the same way I cling to God at 5:00 in the morning when I wake up thinking that maybe Pammy is not going to live forever.

I wonder if someday Sam will end up believing in God. Let's face it, the whole thing is sort of ridiculous. I was talking to Bill Rankin about Pammy, and somehow we ended up talking about this teenage boy in Bill's parish who died recently of bone cancer. I felt really appalled, because the whole family had been fighting so hard and keeping so faithful, and then the kid just died anyway. It just fills me with unspeakable terror, for obvious reasons. And I asked Bill, "What kind of all-merciful God would let that happen?" and Bill just sort of shook his head. I said, "Don't you priests have anything to say for yourselves?" and he said that a God who adores us and is truly and totally merciful and present for us, who will one day bring us home to be with him, is something we *hope* is true, something our faith tells us is true. And I said, "Well, that is not very goddamn much, is it?" and he shook his head. And I said, "Do you think this teenage boy is with God now, in his arms, and if Pammy dies, she'll be with him, too? And that he's taking care of her somehow right now?" And he looked at me sort of apologetically, for a really long time, and then he said, "I don't know." I said. "But what do you *think?*" and he said in this very gentle voice, "I *hope* so."

I don't know what to make of it all. But, as I was writing this just now, Sam went into the living room closet, played a little song on the guitar, and then, just this second, peered around from behind the closet door, babbling absolutely incoherently, grinning at me like some like crazy old Indian holy man.

PAMELA MURRAY DIED AT HOME
IN MILL VALLEY, CALIFORNIA,
ON NOVEMBER 2, 1992.
SHE WAS THIRTY-SEVEN YEARS OLD.

ABOUT THE AUTHOR

Anne Lamott was born in 1954 in San Francisco. After studying at Goucher College, she returned to the Bay Area to write.
In 1980 her first novel, *Hard Laughter*, was published, followed
by *Rosie* (1983), *Joe Jones* (1985), and *All New People* (1989). A
past recipient of a Guggenheim, she has been the book review
columnist for *Mademoiselle* and restaurant critic for *California*
magazine, and has taught writing at UC Davis and at many
other writing conferences throughout the state. She lives in
San Rafael, California, with her son, Sam, now three years old.